Microsoft Office 365
Complete Self-Assessment Guide

The guidance in this Self-Assessment is based on Microsoft Office 365 best practices and standards in business process architecture, design and quality management. The guidance is also based on the professional judgment of the individual collaborators listed in the Acknowledgments.

Notice of rights

Trademarks

Many of the designations used by manufacturers and sellers to distinguish their products are claimed as trademarks. Where those designations appear in this book, and the publisher was aware of a trademark claim, the designations appear as requested by the owner of the trademark. All other product names and services identified throughout this book are used in editorial fashion only and for the benefit of such companies with no intention of infringement of the trademark. No such use, or the use of any trade name, is intended to convey endorsement or other affiliation with this book.

Table of Contents

4

About The Art of Service

The Art of Service, Business Process Architects since 2000, is dedicated to helping stakeholders achieve excellence.

Defining, designing, creating, and implementing a process to solve a stakeholders challenge or meet an objective is the most valuable role… In EVERY group, company, organization and department.

Unless you're talking a one-time, single-use project, there should be a process. Whether that process is managed and implemented by humans, AI, or a combination of the two, it needs to be designed by someone with a complex enough perspective to ask the right questions.

Someone capable of asking the right questions and step back and say, 'What are we really trying to accomplish here? And is there a different way to look at it?'

With The Art of Service's Standard Requirements Self-Assessments, we empower people who can do just that — whether their title is marketer, entrepreneur, manager, salesperson, consultant, Business Process Manager, executive assistant, IT Manager, CIO etc... —they are the people who rule the future. They are people who watch the process as it happens, and ask the right questions to make the process work better.

Contact us when you need any support with this Self-Assessment and any help with templates, blue-prints and examples of standard documents you might need:

http://theartofservice.com
service@theartofservice.com

Acknowledgments

This checklist was developed under the auspices of The Art of Service, chaired by Gerardus Blokdyk.

Representatives from several client companies participated in the preparation of this Self-Assessment.

In addition, we are thankful for the design and printing services provided.

Included Resources - how to access

Included with your purchase of the book is the Microsoft Office 365 Self-Assessment Spreadsheet Dashboard which contains all questions and Self-Assessment areas and auto-generates insights, graphs, and project RACI planning - all with examples to get you started right away.

How? Simply send an email to
access@theartofservice.com
with this books' title in the subject to get the Microsoft Office 365 Self Assessment Tool right away.

You will receive the following contents with New and Updated specific criteria:

• The latest quick edition of the book in PDF

• The latest complete edition of the book in PDF, which criteria correspond to the criteria in...

• The Self-Assessment Excel Dashboard, and...

• Example pre-filled Self-Assessment Excel Dashboard to get familiar with results generation

• In-depth specific Checklists covering the topic

• Project management checklists and templates to assist with implementation

INCLUDES LIFETIME SELF ASSESSMENT UPDATES

Every self assessment comes with Lifetime Updates and Lifetime Free Updated Books. Lifetime Updates is an industry-first feature which allows you to receive verified self assessment updates, ensuring you always have the most accurate information at your fingertips.

Get it now- you will be glad you did - do it now, before you forget.

Send an email to **access@theartofservice.com** with this books' title in the subject to get the Microsoft Office 365 Self Assessment Tool right away.

Your feedback is invaluable to us

If you recently bought this book, we would love to hear from you! You can do this by writing a review on amazon (or the online store where you purchased this book) about your last purchase! As part of our continual service improvement process, we love to hear real client experiences and feedback.

How does it work?
To post a review on Amazon, just log in to your account and click on the Create Your Own Review button (under Customer Reviews) of the relevant product page. You can find examples of product reviews in Amazon. If you purchased from another online store, simply follow their procedures.

What happens when I submit my review?
Once you have submitted your review, send us an email at review@theartofservice.com with the link to your review so we can properly thank you for your feedback.

Purpose of this Self-Assessment

This Self-Assessment has been developed to improve understanding of the requirements and elements of Microsoft Office 365, based on best practices and standards in business process architecture, design and quality management.

It is designed to allow for a rapid Self-Assessment to determine how closely existing management practices and procedures correspond to the elements of the Self-Assessment.

The criteria of requirements and elements of Microsoft Office 365 have been rephrased in the format of a Self-Assessment questionnaire, with a seven-criterion scoring system, as explained in this document.

In this format, even with limited background knowledge of

Microsoft Office 365, a manager can quickly review existing operations to determine how they measure up to the standards. This in turn can serve as the starting point of a 'gap analysis' to identify management tools or system elements that might usefully be implemented in the organization to help improve overall performance.

How to use the Self-Assessment

On the following pages are a series of questions to identify to what extent your Microsoft Office 365 initiative is complete in comparison to the requirements set in standards.

To facilitate answering the questions, there is a space in front of each question to enter a score on a scale of '1' to '5'.

1 Strongly Disagree

2 Disagree

3 Neutral

4 Agree

5 Strongly Agree

Read the question and rate it with the following in front of mind:

'In my belief,
the answer to this question is clearly defined'.

There are two ways in which you can choose to interpret this statement;
1. how aware are you that the answer to the question is clearly defined
2. for more in-depth analysis you can choose to gather

evidence and confirm the answer to the question. This obviously will take more time, most Self-Assessment users opt for the first way to interpret the question and dig deeper later on based on the outcome of the overall Self-Assessment.

A score of '1' would mean that the answer is not clear at all, where a '5' would mean the answer is crystal clear and defined. Leave emtpy when the question is not applicable or you don't want to answer it, you can skip it without affecting your score. Write your score in the space provided.

After you have responded to all the appropriate statements in each section, compute your average score for that section, using the formula provided, and round to the nearest tenth. Then transfer to the corresponding spoke in the Microsoft Office 365 Scorecard on the second next page of the Self-Assessment.

Your completed Microsoft Office 365 Scorecard will give you a clear presentation of which Microsoft Office 365 areas need attention.

Microsoft Office 365
Scorecard Example

Example of how the finalized Scorecard can look like:

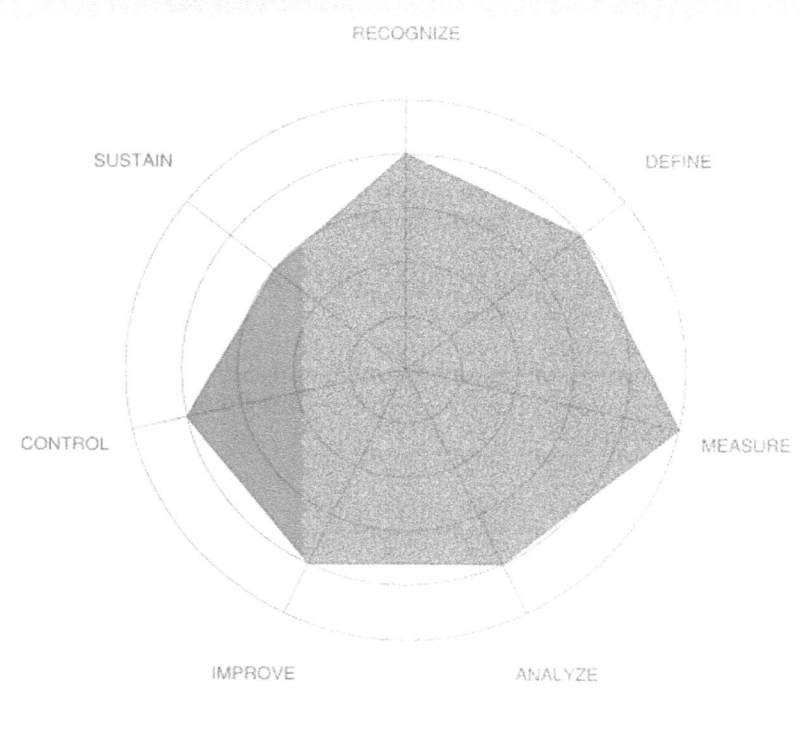

Microsoft Office 365 Scorecard

Your Scores:

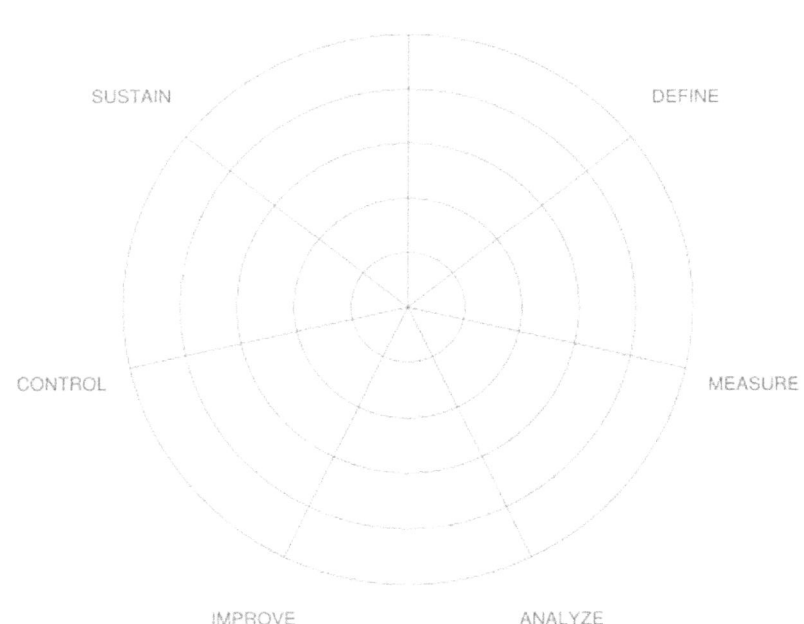

BEGINNING OF THE SELF-ASSESSMENT:

CRITERION #1: RECOGNIZE

INTENT: Be aware of the need for change. Recognize that there is an unfavorable variation, problem or symptom.

In my belief, the answer to this question is clearly defined:

5 Strongly Agree

4 Agree

3 Neutral

2 Disagree

1 Strongly Disagree

1. How are you going to measure success?
<--- Score

2. Can management personnel recognize the monetary benefit of Microsoft Office 365?
<--- Score

3. What problems are you facing and how do you consider Microsoft Office 365 will circumvent those

obstacles?
<--- Score

4. Who defines the rules in relation to any given issue?
<--- Score

5. How do you identify the kinds of information that you will need?
<--- Score

6. What does Microsoft Office 365 success mean to the stakeholders?
<--- Score

7. What kinds of technology will you need?
<--- Score

8. Do you have/need 24-hour access to key personnel?
<--- Score

9. What are the minority interests and what amount of minority interests can be recognized?
<--- Score

10. What do you need to start doing?
<--- Score

11. When a Microsoft Office 365 manager recognizes a problem, what options are available?
<--- Score

12. Does Microsoft Office 365 create potential expectations in other areas that need to be recognized and considered?
<--- Score

13. What kind of information is needed?
<--- Score

14. What else needs to be measured?
<--- Score

15. Who are your key stakeholders who need to sign off?
<--- Score

16. Are there any specific expectations or concerns about the Microsoft Office 365 team, Microsoft Office 365 itself?
<--- Score

17. How much are sponsors, customers, partners, stakeholders involved in Microsoft Office 365? In other words, what are the risks, if Microsoft Office 365 does not deliver successfully?
<--- Score

18. Will Microsoft Office 365 deliverables need to be tested and, if so, by whom?
<--- Score

19. What prevents you from making the changes you know will make you a more effective Microsoft Office 365 leader?
<--- Score

20. Which problem(s) need to be solved?
<--- Score

21. What tools and technologies are needed for a custom Microsoft Office 365 project?
<--- Score

22. Who needs to know about Microsoft Office 365?
<--- Score

23. To what extent would your organization benefit from being recognized as a award recipient?
<--- Score

24. To what extent does each concerned units management team recognize Microsoft Office 365 as an effective investment?
<--- Score

25. Do you know what you need to know about Microsoft Office 365?
<--- Score

26. What vendors make products that address the Microsoft Office 365 needs?
<--- Score

27. Who else hopes to benefit from it?
<--- Score

28. Do you need different information or graphics?
<--- Score

29. Do you need to integrate with several other systems?
<--- Score

30. Do you need to avoid or amend any Microsoft Office 365 activities?
<--- Score

31. Who had the original idea?

<--- Score

32. Will a response program recognize when a crisis occurs and provide some level of response?
<--- Score

33. Will you need to change settings on your mobile devices?
<--- Score

34. Will it solve real problems?
<--- Score

35. How can auditing be a preventative security measure?
<--- Score

36. Are there any revenue recognition issues?
<--- Score

37. Looking at each person individually – does every one have the qualities which are needed to work in this group?
<--- Score

38. How does it fit into your organizational needs and tasks?
<--- Score

39. What should be considered when identifying available resources, constraints, and deadlines?
<--- Score

40. Are controls defined to recognize and contain problems?
<--- Score

41. Why do you need these tools?
<--- Score

42. What is the problem or issue?
<--- Score

43. What would happen if Microsoft Office 365 weren't done?
<--- Score

44. What needs to be done?
<--- Score

45. Who needs what information?
<--- Score

46. As a sponsor, customer or management, how important is it to meet goals, objectives?
<--- Score

47. How are the Microsoft Office 365's objectives aligned to the organization's overall business strategy?
<--- Score

48. Think about the people you identified for your Microsoft Office 365 project and the project responsibilities you would assign to them. what kind of training do you think they would need to perform these responsibilities effectively?
<--- Score

49. What training and capacity building actions are needed to implement proposed reforms?
<--- Score

50. Is it clear when you think of the day ahead of you what activities and tasks you need to complete?
<--- Score

51. How do you assess your Microsoft Office 365 workforce capability and capacity needs, including skills, competencies, and staffing levels?
<--- Score

52. What are the expected benefits of Microsoft Office 365 to the business?
<--- Score

53. What changes are needed?
<--- Score

54. For your Microsoft Office 365 project, identify and describe the business environment, is there more than one layer to the business environment?
<--- Score

55. What are the problems to be solved?
<--- Score

56. So you say you need software, but do you know why?
<--- Score

57. Is the need for organizational change recognized?
<--- Score

58. Are problem definition and motivation clearly presented?
<--- Score

59. Are you dealing with any of the same issues today as yesterday? What can you do about this?
<--- Score

60. What are your needs in relation to Microsoft Office 365 skills, labor, equipment, and markets?
<--- Score

61. Does your organization need more Microsoft Office 365 education?
<--- Score

62. What extra resources will you need?
<--- Score

63. What are the timeframes required to resolve each of the issues/problems?
<--- Score

64. How do you take a forward-looking perspective in identifying Microsoft Office 365 research related to market response and models?
<--- Score

65. What are the business objectives to be achieved with Microsoft Office 365?
<--- Score

66. Are your goals realistic? Do you need to redefine your problem? Perhaps the problem has changed or maybe you have reached your goal and need to set a new one?
<--- Score

67. Should you invest in industry-recognized qualications?

<--- Score

68. What situation(s) led to this Microsoft Office 365 Self Assessment?
<--- Score

69. Are employees recognized or rewarded for performance that demonstrates the highest levels of integrity?
<--- Score

70. What is the smallest subset of the problem you can usefully solve?
<--- Score

71. What information do users need?
<--- Score

72. Consider your own Microsoft Office 365 project, what types of organizational problems do you think might be causing or affecting your problem, based on the work done so far?
<--- Score

73. Are there Microsoft Office 365 problems defined?
<--- Score

74. Will new equipment/products be required to facilitate Microsoft Office 365 delivery, for example is new software needed?
<--- Score

75. Are there recognized Microsoft Office 365 problems?
<--- Score

Add up total points for this section:
_____ = Total points for this section

Divided by: _____ (number of
statements answered) = _____
Average score for this section

Transfer your score to the Microsoft
Office 365 Index at the beginning of the
Self-Assessment.

CRITERION #2: DEFINE:

In my belief, the answer to this question is clearly defined:

5 Strongly Agree

4 Agree

3 Neutral

2 Disagree

1 Strongly Disagree

1. What are the record-keeping requirements of Microsoft Office 365 activities?
<--- Score

2. Is there a critical path to deliver Microsoft Office 365 results?
<--- Score

3. Are there different segments of customers?

<--- Score

4. Has a high-level 'as is' process map been completed, verified and validated?
<--- Score

5. Is full participation by members in regularly held team meetings guaranteed?
<--- Score

6. What would be the goal or target for a Microsoft Office 365's improvement team?
<--- Score

7. Is the team adequately staffed with the desired cross-functionality? If not, what additional resources are available to the team?
<--- Score

8. Are customers identified and high impact areas defined?
<--- Score

9. What was the context?
<--- Score

10. Have all basic functions of Microsoft Office 365 been defined?
<--- Score

11. What is the scope of Microsoft Office 365?
<--- Score

12. Are accountability and ownership for Microsoft Office 365 clearly defined?
<--- Score

13. How and when will the baselines be defined?
<--- Score

14. Is there a completed, verified, and validated high-level 'as is' (not 'should be' or 'could be') business process map?
<--- Score

15. What are the dynamics of the communication plan?
<--- Score

16. What sources do you use to gather information for a Microsoft Office 365 study?
<--- Score

17. Is Internet access required for Office?
<--- Score

18. What are the compelling business reasons for embarking on Microsoft Office 365?
<--- Score

19. Is the current 'as is' process being followed? If not, what are the discrepancies?
<--- Score

20. Is it clearly defined in and to your organization what you do?
<--- Score

21. Has a team charter been developed and communicated?
<--- Score

22. Who defines (or who defined) the rules and roles?
<--- Score

23. How does the Microsoft Office 365 manager ensure against scope creep?
<--- Score

24. What is the scope of the Microsoft Office 365 effort?
<--- Score

25. When are meeting minutes sent out? Who is on the distribution list?
<--- Score

26. What are the tasks and definitions?
<--- Score

27. What is the definition of success?
<--- Score

28. How was the 'as is' process map developed, reviewed, verified and validated?
<--- Score

29. What happens if Microsoft Office 365's scope changes?
<--- Score

30. What baselines are required to be defined and managed?
<--- Score

31. Is the team equipped with available and reliable resources?
<--- Score

32. Is the scope of Microsoft Office 365 defined?
<--- Score

33. Will team members regularly document their Microsoft Office 365 work?
<--- Score

34. Who are the Microsoft Office 365 improvement team members, including Management Leads and Coaches?
<--- Score

35. Have specific policy objectives been defined?
<--- Score

36. Are required metrics defined, what are they?
<--- Score

37. Are task requirements clearly defined?
<--- Score

38. Has anyone else (internal or external to the organization) attempted to solve this problem or a similar one before? If so, what knowledge can be leveraged from these previous efforts?
<--- Score

39. Who is gathering Microsoft Office 365 information?
<--- Score

40. How do you keep key subject matter experts in the loop?
<--- Score

41. How do you hand over Microsoft Office 365 context?
<--- Score

42. For selected date ranges, in a way that complies with all requirements and labor rules (leaving shifts unassigned if necessary)?
<--- Score

43. What is out of scope?
<--- Score

44. Does the scope remain the same?
<--- Score

45. Has/have the customer(s) been identified?
<--- Score

46. Is the Microsoft Office 365 scope complete and appropriately sized?
<--- Score

47. What are the rough order estimates on cost savings/opportunities that Microsoft Office 365 brings?
<--- Score

48. Are team charters developed?
<--- Score

49. What customer feedback methods were used to solicit their input?
<--- Score

50. What is the scope?
<--- Score

51. Does the organization have any specific reports (defined format) that must exist at the time of go-live?
<--- Score

52. Are there any constraints known that bear on the ability to perform Microsoft Office 365 work? How is the team addressing them?
<--- Score

53. What is the context?
<--- Score

54. Is the required technology available in house ?
<--- Score

55. Is the Microsoft Office 365 scope manageable?
<--- Score

56. Is Microsoft Office 365 required?
<--- Score

57. What system do you use for gathering Microsoft Office 365 information?
<--- Score

58. When was the Microsoft Office 365 start date?
<--- Score

59. Is there a completed SIPOC representation, describing the Suppliers, Inputs, Process, Outputs, and Customers?
<--- Score

60. What key business process output measure(s) does

Microsoft Office 365 leverage and how?
<--- Score

61. How often are the team meetings?
<--- Score

62. When is the estimated completion date?
<--- Score

63. Are improvement team members fully trained on Microsoft Office 365?
<--- Score

64. Does the vendor software provide case alerts?
<--- Score

65. How would you define the culture at your organization, how susceptible is it to Microsoft Office 365 changes?
<--- Score

66. Are roles and responsibilities formally defined?
<--- Score

67. How will the Microsoft Office 365 team and the organization measure complete success of Microsoft Office 365?
<--- Score

68. Have the customer needs been translated into specific, measurable requirements? How?
<--- Score

69. What is out-of-scope initially?
<--- Score

70. How can the value of Microsoft Office 365 be defined?
<--- Score

71. What critical content must be communicated – who, what, when, where, and how?
<--- Score

72. How do you gather Microsoft Office 365 requirements?
<--- Score

73. What are the Roles and Responsibilities for each team member and its leadership? Where is this documented?
<--- Score

74. Are business processes mapped?
<--- Score

75. Are resources adequate for the scope?
<--- Score

76. Are different versions of process maps needed to account for the different types of inputs?
<--- Score

77. Scope of sensitive information?
<--- Score

78. Are audit criteria, scope, frequency and methods defined?
<--- Score

79. Why are you doing Microsoft Office 365 and what is the scope?

<--- Score

80. Does the team have regular meetings?
<--- Score

81. Is the team formed and are team leaders (Coaches and Management Leads) assigned?
<--- Score

82. How is the team tracking and documenting its work?
<--- Score

83. Has everyone on the team, including the team leaders, been properly trained?
<--- Score

84. Has the direction changed at all during the course of Microsoft Office 365? If so, when did it change and why?
<--- Score

85. What Microsoft Office 365 requirements should be gathered?
<--- Score

86. What is in the scope and what is not in scope?
<--- Score

87. What scope to assess?
<--- Score

88. Do you all define Microsoft Office 365 in the same way?
<--- Score

89. If substitutes have been appointed, have they been briefed on the Microsoft Office 365 goals and received regular communications as to the progress to date?
<--- Score

90. What specifically is the problem? Where does it occur? When does it occur? What is its extent?
<--- Score

91. Are approval levels defined for contracts and supplements to contracts?
<--- Score

92. Is Microsoft Office 365 linked to key business goals and objectives?
<--- Score

93. Do the problem and goal statements meet the SMART criteria (specific, measurable, attainable, relevant, and time-bound)?
<--- Score

94. Is there regularly 100% attendance at the team meetings? If not, have appointed substitutes attended to preserve cross-functionality and full representation?
<--- Score

95. Is data collected and displayed to better understand customer(s) critical needs and requirements.
<--- Score

96. Is there a Microsoft Office 365 management charter, including business case, problem and

goal statements, scope, milestones, roles and responsibilities, communication plan?
<--- Score

97. Is scope creep really all bad news?
<--- Score

98. What constraints exist that might impact the team?
<--- Score

99. Has your scope been defined?
<--- Score

100. What defines best in class?
<--- Score

101. Are customer(s) identified and segmented according to their different needs and requirements?
<--- Score

102. How will variation in the actual durations of each activity be dealt with to ensure that the expected Microsoft Office 365 results are met?
<--- Score

103. How many system managers can be defined?
<--- Score

104. Have all of the relationships been defined properly?
<--- Score

105. In what way can you redefine the criteria of choice clients have in your category in your favor?
<--- Score

106. How do you think the partners involved in Microsoft Office 365 would have defined success?
<--- Score

107. What is in scope?
<--- Score

108. Has the Microsoft Office 365 work been fairly and/or equitably divided and delegated among team members who are qualified and capable to perform the work? Has everyone contributed?
<--- Score

109. Will team members perform Microsoft Office 365 work when assigned and in a timely fashion?
<--- Score

110. Has a project plan, Gantt chart, or similar been developed/completed?
<--- Score

111. How do you manage scope?
<--- Score

112. Is a fully trained team formed, supported, and committed to work on the Microsoft Office 365 improvements?
<--- Score

113. What are the boundaries of the scope? What is in bounds and what is not? What is the start point? What is the stop point?
<--- Score

114. How did the Microsoft Office 365 manager

receive input to the development of a Microsoft Office 365 improvement plan and the estimated completion dates/times of each activity?
<--- Score

115. Is Microsoft Office 365 currently on schedule according to the plan?
<--- Score

116. Has the improvement team collected the 'voice of the customer' (obtained feedback – qualitative and quantitative)?
<--- Score

117. Is the improvement team aware of the different versions of a process: what they think it is vs. what it actually is vs. what it should be vs. what it could be?
<--- Score

118. Is the team sponsored by a champion or business leader?
<--- Score

Add up total points for this section:
_ _ _ _ _ = Total points for this section

Divided by: _ _ _ _ _ _ (number of statements answered) = _ _ _ _ _ _
Average score for this section

Transfer your score to the Microsoft Office 365 Index at the beginning of the Self-Assessment.

CRITERION #3: MEASURE:

INTENT: Gather the correct data. Measure the current performance and evolution of the situation.

In my belief, the answer to this question is clearly defined:

5 Strongly Agree

4 Agree

3 Neutral

2 Disagree

1 Strongly Disagree

1. What methods are feasible and acceptable to estimate the impact of reforms?
<--- Score

2. Have the concerns of stakeholders to help identify and define potential barriers been obtained and analyzed?
<--- Score

3. What disadvantage does this cause for the user?
<--- Score

4. How will success or failure be measured?
<--- Score

5. Does your organization systematically track and analyze outcomes related for accountability and quality improvement?
<--- Score

6. What are your key Microsoft Office 365 indicators that you will measure, analyze and track?
<--- Score

7. How do you do risk analysis of rare, cascading, catastrophic events?
<--- Score

8. Are there measurements based on task performance?
<--- Score

9. What potential environmental factors impact the Microsoft Office 365 effort?
<--- Score

10. What is an unallowable cost?
<--- Score

11. Are missed Microsoft Office 365 opportunities costing your organization money?
<--- Score

12. Can you do Microsoft Office 365 without complex (expensive) analysis?

<--- Score

13. Did you tackle the cause or the symptom?
<--- Score

14. What causes investor action?
<--- Score

15. Is data collected on key measures that were identified?
<--- Score

16. Are you aware of what could cause a problem?
<--- Score

17. How is the value delivered by Microsoft Office 365 being measured?
<--- Score

18. What key measures identified indicate the performance of the business process?
<--- Score

19. Which measures and indicators matter?
<--- Score

20. Does Microsoft Office 365 analysis isolate the fundamental causes of problems?
<--- Score

21. What are the process impacts?
<--- Score

22. Have all non-recommended alternatives been analyzed in sufficient detail?
<--- Score

23. How do you measure variability?
<--- Score

24. Is Process Variation Displayed/Communicated?
<--- Score

25. What harm might be caused?
<--- Score

26. What could cause you to change course?
<--- Score

27. Is long term and short term variability accounted for?
<--- Score

28. What data was collected (past, present, future/ongoing)?
<--- Score

29. Have you made assumptions about the shape of the future, particularly its impact on your customers and competitors?
<--- Score

30. Was a data collection plan established?
<--- Score

31. How will you measure success?
<--- Score

32. What are the costs of reform?
<--- Score

33. Which stakeholder characteristics are analyzed?

<--- Score

34. Who participated in the data collection for measurements?
<--- Score

35. Are the measurements objective?
<--- Score

36. How do you control the overall costs of your work processes?
<--- Score

37. How do you identify and analyze stakeholders and their interests?
<--- Score

38. How do you measure efficient delivery of Microsoft Office 365 services?
<--- Score

39. How will the cost of Office 365 be charged (annually, monthly)?
<--- Score

40. How do you focus on what is right -not who is right?
<--- Score

41. Are losses documented, analyzed, and remedial processes developed to prevent future losses?
<--- Score

42. How to cause the change?
<--- Score

43. Have the types of risks that may impact Microsoft Office 365 been identified and analyzed?
<--- Score

44. Are key measures identified and agreed upon?
<--- Score

45. What relevant entities could be measured?
<--- Score

46. How do you measure success?
<--- Score

47. How will effects be measured?
<--- Score

48. What particular quality tools did the team find helpful in establishing measurements?
<--- Score

49. What evidence is there and what is measured?
<--- Score

50. How will you measure your Microsoft Office 365 effectiveness?
<--- Score

51. What do you measure and why?
<--- Score

52. How do you aggregate measures across priorities?
<--- Score

53. How do your measurements capture actionable Microsoft Office 365 information for use in exceeding your customers expectations and securing your

customers engagement?

<--- Score

54. What will the cost for Office 365 be to departments?

<--- Score

55. Is data collection planned and executed?

<--- Score

56. What are the uncertainties surrounding estimates of impact?

<--- Score

57. Do you effectively measure and reward individual and team performance?

<--- Score

58. How large is the gap between current performance and the customer-specified (goal) performance?

<--- Score

59. Have you found any 'ground fruit' or 'low-hanging fruit' for immediate remedies to the gap in performance?

<--- Score

60. What would be a real cause for concern?

<--- Score

61. What are your key Microsoft Office 365 organizational performance measures, including key short and longer-term financial measures?

<--- Score

62. Why do the measurements/indicators matter?
<--- Score

63. What is the impact for your O365 account if your active directory or network password expired or changed?
<--- Score

64. Are high impact defects defined and identified in the business process?
<--- Score

65. Have changes been properly/adequately analyzed for effect?
<--- Score

66. What causes extra work or rework?
<--- Score

67. Can you measure the return on analysis?
<--- Score

68. How do you know that any Microsoft Office 365 analysis is complete and comprehensive?
<--- Score

69. What are the types and number of measures to use?
<--- Score

70. What causes innovation to fail or succeed in your organization?
<--- Score

71. Do you aggressively reward and promote the people who have the biggest impact on creating

excellent Microsoft Office 365 services/products?
<--- Score

72. How frequently do you track Microsoft Office 365 measures?
<--- Score

73. How can you measure Microsoft Office 365 in a systematic way?
<--- Score

74. Why do you expend time and effort to implement measurement, for whom?
<--- Score

75. Is a solid data collection plan established that includes measurement systems analysis?
<--- Score

76. What are the agreed upon definitions of the high impact areas, defect(s), unit(s), and opportunities that will figure into the process capability metrics?
<--- Score

77. How will measures be used to manage and adapt?
<--- Score

78. How do you stay flexible and focused to recognize larger Microsoft Office 365 results?
<--- Score

79. Are process variation components displayed/communicated using suitable charts, graphs, plots?
<--- Score

80. What is the right balance of time and resources

between investigation, analysis, and discussion and dissemination?
<--- Score

81. How can you measure the performance?
<--- Score

82. Who should receive measurement reports?
<--- Score

83. How do you measure lifecycle phases?
<--- Score

84. What measurements are possible, practicable and meaningful?
<--- Score

85. Are you taking your company in the direction of better and revenue or cheaper and cost?
<--- Score

86. Is key measure data collection planned and executed, process variation displayed and communicated and performance baselined?
<--- Score

87. Are the units of measure consistent?
<--- Score

88. Is it possible to estimate the impact of unanticipated complexity such as wrong or failed assumptions, feedback, etc. on proposed reforms?
<--- Score

89. What are your customers expectations and measures?

<--- Score

90. How is progress measured?
<--- Score

91. When does lifetime benefits overtake lifetime costs?
<--- Score

92. What cost savings can be expected from this migration to offset the estimated internal costs to change all our stationery, websites, applications, business cards, consumer literature, reports, etc.?
<--- Score

93. What could cause delays in the schedule?
<--- Score

94. Are there any easy-to-implement alternatives to Microsoft Office 365? Sometimes other solutions are available that do not require the cost implications of a full-blown project?
<--- Score

95. What are the key input variables? What are the key process variables? What are the key output variables?
<--- Score

96. Is there a Performance Baseline?
<--- Score

97. Where is it measured?
<--- Score

98. What is the minimal cost to attain a certain system?

<--- Score

99. What causes mismanagement?
<--- Score

100. Expected cost of the overall project ($)?
<--- Score

101. Does Microsoft Office 365 analysis show the relationships among important Microsoft Office 365 factors?
<--- Score

102. Among the Microsoft Office 365 product and service cost to be estimated, which is considered hardest to estimate?
<--- Score

103. How is performance measured?
<--- Score

104. How are measurements made?
<--- Score

105. What charts has the team used to display the components of variation in the process?
<--- Score

106. Initial software purchase costs -what is included?
<--- Score

107. Do staff have the necessary skills to collect, analyze, and report data?
<--- Score

108. What measurements are being captured?
<--- Score

109. What has the team done to assure the stability and accuracy of the measurement process?
<--- Score

110. Does Microsoft Office 365 systematically track and analyze outcomes for accountability and quality improvement?
<--- Score

111. The approach of traditional Microsoft Office 365 works for detail complexity but is focused on a systematic approach rather than an understanding of the nature of systems themselves, what approach will permit your organization to deal with the kind of unpredictable emergent behaviors that dynamic complexity can introduce?
<--- Score

112. How will your organization measure success?
<--- Score

113. What is measured? Why?
<--- Score

114. Does the Microsoft Office 365 task fit the client's priorities?
<--- Score

115. Is the solution cost-effective?
<--- Score

Add up total points for this section:
_ _ _ _ _ = Total points for this section

Divided by: _____ (number of
statements answered) = _____
Average score for this section

Transfer your score to the Microsoft
Office 365 Index at the beginning of the
Self-Assessment.

CRITERION #4: ANALYZE:

INTENT: Analyze causes, assumptions and hypotheses.

In my belief, the answer to this question is clearly defined:

5 Strongly Agree

4 Agree

3 Neutral

2 Disagree

1 Strongly Disagree

1. What process should you select for improvement?
<--- Score

2. Do your leaders quickly bounce back from setbacks?
<--- Score

3. What kinds of data and technical information do you review?
<--- Score

4. Where is Microsoft Office 365 data gathered?
<--- Score

5. Is Data and process analysis, root cause analysis and quantifying the gap/opportunity in place?
<--- Score

6. How do you use Microsoft Office 365 data and information to support organizational decision making and innovation?
<--- Score

7. How do you implement and manage your work processes to ensure that they meet design requirements?
<--- Score

8. What is the requirement for bringing in your existing data?
<--- Score

9. What quality tools were used to get through the analyze phase?
<--- Score

10. What are your best practices for minimizing Microsoft Office 365 project risk, while demonstrating incremental value and quick wins throughout the Microsoft Office 365 project lifecycle?
<--- Score

11. A compounding model resolution with available relevant data can often provide insight towards a solution methodology; which Microsoft Office 365 models, tools and techniques are necessary?

<--- Score

12. What is the cost of poor quality as supported by the team's analysis?
<--- Score

13. What are your current levels and trends in key Microsoft Office 365 measures or indicators of product and process performance that are important to and directly serve your customers?
<--- Score

14. What functions/data are needed?
<--- Score

15. How do you get data for performance reviews?
<--- Score

16. What are the data attributes and relationships?
<--- Score

17. What are the best opportunities for value improvement?
<--- Score

18. Have the problem and goal statements been updated to reflect the additional knowledge gained from the analyze phase?
<--- Score

19. Will the Licensing Database and Software System be required to integrate with any external systems?
<--- Score

20. Were any designed experiments used to generate

additional insight into the data analysis?
<--- Score

21. Were there any improvement opportunities identified from the process analysis?
<--- Score

22. What are your key performance measures or indicators and in-process measures for the control and improvement of your Microsoft Office 365 processes?
<--- Score

23. What are the revised rough estimates of the financial savings/opportunity for Microsoft Office 365 improvements?
<--- Score

24. Have any additional benefits been identified that will result from closing all or most of the gaps?
<--- Score

25. How often will data be collected for measures?
<--- Score

26. Was a detailed process map created to amplify critical steps of the 'as is' business process?
<--- Score

27. What tools were used to generate the list of possible causes?
<--- Score

28. What other jobs or tasks affect the performance of the steps in the Microsoft Office 365 process?
<--- Score

29. Is the performance gap determined?
<--- Score

30. What is the purpose of the database?
<--- Score

31. What are your Microsoft Office 365 processes?
<--- Score

32. Where is the data coming from to measure compliance?
<--- Score

33. What successful thing are you doing today that may be blinding you to new growth opportunities?
<--- Score

34. What controls do you have in place to protect data?
<--- Score

35. How do mission and objectives affect the Microsoft Office 365 processes of your organization?
<--- Score

36. Are my documents stored in OneDrive also available offline?
<--- Score

37. What is the OneDrive for Business file storage limit?
<--- Score

38. What were the financial benefits resulting from any 'ground fruit or low-hanging fruit' (quick fixes)?

<--- Score

39. An organizationally feasible system request is one that considers the mission, goals and objectives of the organization. Key questions are: is the Microsoft Office 365 solution request practical and will it solve a problem or take advantage of an opportunity to achieve company goals?
<--- Score

40. What conclusions were drawn from the team's data collection and analysis? How did the team reach these conclusions?
<--- Score

41. Can you add value to the current Microsoft Office 365 decision-making process (largely qualitative) by incorporating uncertainty modeling (more quantitative)?
<--- Score

42. Do your employees have the opportunity to do what they do best everyday?
<--- Score

43. What does the data say about the performance of the business process?
<--- Score

44. What other organizational variables, such as reward systems or communication systems, affect the performance of this Microsoft Office 365 process?
<--- Score

45. What methods do you use to gather Microsoft Office 365 data?

<--- Score

46. Did any additional data need to be collected?
<--- Score

47. How does Office 365 affect data retention practices?
<--- Score

48. Think about the functions involved in your Microsoft Office 365 project, what processes flow from these functions?
<--- Score

49. What tools were used to narrow the list of possible causes?
<--- Score

50. Did any value-added analysis or 'lean thinking' take place to identify some of the gaps shown on the 'as is' process map?
<--- Score

51. What is your organizations process which leads to recognition of value generation?
<--- Score

52. Think about some of the processes you undertake within your organization, which do you own?
<--- Score

53. Does the organization have a preferred payment processing system that will be used with this new system?
<--- Score

54. Is the gap/opportunity displayed and communicated in financial terms?
<--- Score

55. What were the crucial 'moments of truth' on the process map?
<--- Score

56. What will drive Microsoft Office 365 change?
<--- Score

57. How is the way you as the leader think and process information affecting your organizational culture?
<--- Score

58. Are gaps between current performance and the goal performance identified?
<--- Score

59. How was the detailed process map generated, verified, and validated?
<--- Score

60. Who will help with the Access database conversions when new versions are pushed out?
<--- Score

61. How is Microsoft Office 365 data gathered?
<--- Score

62. Were Pareto charts (or similar) used to portray the 'heavy hitters' (or key sources of variation)?
<--- Score

63. Is the Microsoft Office 365 process severely broken such that a re-design is necessary?

<--- Score

64. Are Microsoft Office 365 changes recognized early enough to be approved through the regular process?
<--- Score

65. What Microsoft Office 365 data do you gather or use now?
<--- Score

66. Was a cause-and-effect diagram used to explore the different types of causes (or sources of variation)?
<--- Score

67. Do several people in different organizational units assist with the Microsoft Office 365 process?
<--- Score

68. Record-keeping requirements flow from the records needed as inputs, outputs, controls and for transformation of a Microsoft Office 365 process. Are the records needed as inputs to the Microsoft Office 365 process available?
<--- Score

69. What are your current levels and trends in key measures or indicators of Microsoft Office 365 product and process performance that are important to and directly serve your customers? How do these results compare with the performance of your competitors and other organizations with similar offerings?
<--- Score

70. How do you select and use comparative data and information?

<--- Score

71. How does the organization define, manage, and improve its Microsoft Office 365 processes?
<--- Score

72. Do you, as a leader, bounce back quickly from setbacks?
<--- Score

73. What data is gathered?
<--- Score

74. The problem of personal data in cloud computing: what information is regulated?
<--- Score

75. What did the team gain from developing a sub-process map?
<--- Score

76. Do your contracts/agreements contain data security obligations?
<--- Score

77. What input data is available to the database?
<--- Score

78. How do you identify specific Microsoft Office 365 investment opportunities and emerging trends?
<--- Score

79. Is the suppliers process defined and controlled?
<--- Score

80. How do you open file on shared drive?

<--- Score

81. Dropbox, Google Drive, OneDrive?
<--- Score

82. How do you promote understanding that opportunity for improvement is not criticism of the status quo, or the people who created the status quo?
<--- Score

83. Is the required Microsoft Office 365 data gathered?
<--- Score

84. How do your work systems and key work processes relate to and capitalize on your core competencies?
<--- Score

85. How do you measure the operational performance of your key work systems and processes, including productivity, cycle time, and other appropriate measures of process effectiveness, efficiency, and innovation?
<--- Score

86. Identify an operational issue in your organization. for example, could a particular task be done more quickly or more efficiently by Microsoft Office 365?
<--- Score

87. What is happening with our current file storage (in home directories and shared drives)?
<--- Score

Add up total points for this section:
_ _ _ _ _ = Total points for this section

Divided by: _____ (number of statements answered) = _____ Average score for this section

Transfer your score to the Microsoft Office 365 Index at the beginning of the Self-Assessment.

CRITERION #5: IMPROVE:

INTENT: Develop a practical solution. Innovate, establish and test the solution and to measure the results.

In my belief, the answer to this question is clearly defined:

5 Strongly Agree

4 Agree

3 Neutral

2 Disagree

1 Strongly Disagree

1. How does the solution remove the key sources of issues discovered in the analyze phase?
<--- Score

2. Does it have the capacity to handle the solution?
<--- Score

3. When you map the key players in your own work and the types/domains of relationships with them,

which relationships do you find easy and which challenging, and why?
<--- Score

4. Who should evaluate software?
<--- Score

5. Why improve in the first place?
<--- Score

6. What is the risk?
<--- Score

7. What attendant changes will need to be made to ensure that the solution is successful?
<--- Score

8. What lessons, if any, from a pilot were incorporated into the design of the full-scale solution?
<--- Score

9. Are improved process ('should be') maps modified based on pilot data and analysis?
<--- Score

10. What actually has to improve and by how much?
<--- Score

11. Is supporting Microsoft Office 365 documentation required?
<--- Score

12. Was a pilot designed for the proposed solution(s)?
<--- Score

13. Are possible solutions generated and tested?

<--- Score

14. Risk events: what are the things that could go wrong?
<--- Score

15. How do you measure progress and evaluate training effectiveness?
<--- Score

16. If you could go back in time five years, what decision would you make differently? What is your best guess as to what decision you're making today you might regret five years from now?
<--- Score

17. How do you keep improving Microsoft Office 365?
<--- Score

18. Is there a cost/benefit analysis of optimal solution(s)?
<--- Score

19. Is pilot data collected and analyzed?
<--- Score

20. What are the implications of the one critical Microsoft Office 365 decision 10 minutes, 10 months, and 10 years from now?
<--- Score

21. Is the solution technically practical?
<--- Score

22. Can you identify any significant risks or exposures to Microsoft Office 365 third- parties (vendors, service

providers, alliance partners etc) that concern you?
<--- Score

23. For decision problems, how do you develop a decision statement?
<--- Score

24. What is the team's contingency plan for potential problems occurring in implementation?
<--- Score

25. Are risk triggers captured?
<--- Score

26. What resources are required for the improvement efforts?
<--- Score

27. Are the best solutions selected?
<--- Score

28. Is a solution implementation plan established, including schedule/work breakdown structure, resources, risk management plan, cost/budget, and control plan?
<--- Score

29. How will the organization know that the solution worked?
<--- Score

30. What are your current levels and trends in key measures or indicators of workforce and leader development?
<--- Score

31. How customizable is the solution?
<--- Score

32. What tools were used to evaluate the potential solutions?
<--- Score

33. Does your organization currently have a preferred document management system of choice?
<--- Score

34. How can you improve Microsoft Office 365?
<--- Score

35. Can the solution be designed and implemented within an acceptable time period?
<--- Score

36. Is the scope clearly documented?
<--- Score

37. Will the controls trigger any other risks?
<--- Score

38. How do the Microsoft Office 365 results compare with the performance of your competitors and other organizations with similar offerings?
<--- Score

39. Are you assessing Microsoft Office 365 and risk?
<--- Score

40. Is a contingency plan established?
<--- Score

41. How do you improve your likelihood of success ?
<--- Score

42. How will the team or the process owner(s) monitor the implementation plan to see that it is working as intended?
<--- Score

43. Which of the recognised risks out of all risks can be most likely transferred?
<--- Score

44. How do you measure risk?
<--- Score

45. What improvements have been achieved?
<--- Score

46. How do you manage and improve your Microsoft Office 365 work systems to deliver customer value and achieve organizational success and sustainability?
<--- Score

47. What communications are necessary to support the implementation of the solution?
<--- Score

48. Who controls key decisions that will be made?
<--- Score

49. How significant is the improvement in the eyes of the end user?
<--- Score

50. Is the measure of success for Microsoft Office 365 understandable to a variety of people?

<--- Score

51. To what extent does management recognize Microsoft Office 365 as a tool to increase the results?
<--- Score

52. How will you know that you have improved?
<--- Score

53. How do you go about comparing Microsoft Office 365 approaches/solutions?
<--- Score

54. Are new and improved process ('should be') maps developed?
<--- Score

55. How will you know when its improved?
<--- Score

56. Is there a high likelihood that any recommendations will achieve their intended results?
<--- Score

57. Explorations of the frontiers of Microsoft Office 365 will help you build influence, improve Microsoft Office 365, optimize decision making, and sustain change, what is your approach?
<--- Score

58. Who will be responsible for making the decisions to include or exclude requested changes once Microsoft Office 365 is underway?
<--- Score

59. How will you know that a change is an

improvement?
<--- Score

60. What do you want to improve?
<--- Score

61. How did the team generate the list of possible solutions?
<--- Score

62. Can you use ports other than 993 for imap to connect to microsoft hosted exchange server?
<--- Score

63. How does the team improve its work?
<--- Score

64. What went well, what should change, what can improve?
<--- Score

65. Who are the people involved in developing and implementing Microsoft Office 365?
<--- Score

66. Is the optimal solution selected based on testing and analysis?
<--- Score

67. How can you improve performance?
<--- Score

68. What is Microsoft Office 365's impact on utilizing the best solution(s)?
<--- Score

69. Which users will have the right to the premium and expensive solution, who will have to settle for the basic version?

<--- Score

70. Risk factors: what are the characteristics of Microsoft Office 365 that make it risky?

<--- Score

71. How do you improve Microsoft Office 365 service perception, and satisfaction?

<--- Score

72. Do those selected for the Microsoft Office 365 team have a good general understanding of what Microsoft Office 365 is all about?

<--- Score

73. Who will be responsible for documenting the Microsoft Office 365 requirements in detail?

<--- Score

74. Describe the design of the pilot and what tests were conducted, if any?

<--- Score

75. What is the implementation plan?

<--- Score

76. What error proofing will be done to address some of the discrepancies observed in the 'as is' process?

<--- Score

77. What is the Microsoft Office 365's sustainability risk?

<--- Score

78. What tools were most useful during the improve phase?
<--- Score

79. How do you link measurement and risk?
<--- Score

80. What does the 'should be' process map/design look like?
<--- Score

81. Risk Identification: What are the possible risk events your organization faces in relation to Microsoft Office 365?
<--- Score

82. Were any criteria developed to assist the team in testing and evaluating potential solutions?
<--- Score

83. Are there any constraints (technical, political, cultural, or otherwise) that would inhibit certain solutions?
<--- Score

84. Is the implementation plan designed?
<--- Score

85. Where will your email and documents be stored once you are using Office 365?
<--- Score

86. What can you do to improve?
<--- Score

87. How will you measure the results?

<--- Score

88. What practices helps your organization to develop its capacity to recognize patterns?

<--- Score

89. In the past few months, what is the smallest change you have made that has had the biggest positive result? What was it about that small change that produced the large return?

<--- Score

90. What is under development?

<--- Score

91. Can you use Office 365 ProPlus with a partner-hosted solution?

<--- Score

92. How can skill-level changes improve Microsoft Office 365?

<--- Score

93. What to do with the results or outcomes of measurements?

<--- Score

94. What is the magnitude of the improvements?

<--- Score

95. Is the proposed technology or solution practical?

<--- Score

96. Who controls the risk?

<--- Score

97. What tools were used to tap into the creativity and encourage 'outside the box' thinking?
<--- Score

98. What were the underlying assumptions on the cost-benefit analysis?
<--- Score

99. Who will be using the results of the measurement activities?
<--- Score

100. Is there a small-scale pilot for proposed improvement(s)? What conclusions were drawn from the outcomes of a pilot?
<--- Score

101. For estimation problems, how do you develop an estimation statement?
<--- Score

102. The alternative solutions you are exploring?
<--- Score

103. How do you measure improved Microsoft Office 365 service perception, and satisfaction?
<--- Score

104. Does the goal represent a desired result that can be measured?
<--- Score

105. How do you define the solutions' scope?
<--- Score

106. How do you improve productivity?
<--- Score

107. What needs improvement? Why?
<--- Score

Add up total points for this section:
_ _ _ _ _ = Total points for this section

Divided by: _ _ _ _ _ _ (number of
statements answered) = _ _ _ _ _ _
Average score for this section

Transfer your score to the Microsoft
Office 365 Index at the beginning of the
Self-Assessment.

CRITERION #6: CONTROL:

INTENT: Implement the practical solution. Maintain the performance and correct possible complications.

In my belief, the answer to this question is clearly defined:

5 Strongly Agree

4 Agree

3 Neutral

2 Disagree

1 Strongly Disagree

1. What are the key elements of your Microsoft Office 365 performance improvement system, including your evaluation, organizational learning, and innovation processes?
<--- Score

2. How will the process owner and team be able to hold the gains?
<--- Score

3. Has the improved process and its steps been standardized?
<--- Score

4. How will input, process, and output variables be checked to detect for sub-optimal conditions?
<--- Score

5. How will the day-to-day responsibilities for monitoring and continual improvement be transferred from the improvement team to the process owner?
<--- Score

6. What are you attempting to measure/monitor?
<--- Score

7. How can you best use all of your knowledge repositories to enhance learning and sharing?
<--- Score

8. Act/Adjust: What Do you Need to Do Differently?
<--- Score

9. Will your goals reflect your program budget?
<--- Score

10. Who will be in control?
<--- Score

11. Is a response plan in place for when the input, process, or output measures indicate an 'out-of-control' condition?
<--- Score

12. How will you measure your QA plan's effectiveness?
<--- Score

13. What should the next improvement project be that is related to Microsoft Office 365?
<--- Score

14. Does the Microsoft Office 365 performance meet the customer's requirements?
<--- Score

15. Does an information system plan exist?
<--- Score

16. What other areas of the organization might benefit from the Microsoft Office 365 team's improvements, knowledge, and learning?
<--- Score

17. Is there a control plan in place for sustaining improvements (short and long-term)?
<--- Score

18. Does Microsoft Office 365 appropriately measure and monitor risk?
<--- Score

19. Is a response plan established and deployed?
<--- Score

20. Are operating procedures consistent?
<--- Score

21. Does job training on the documented procedures need to be part of the process team's education and

training?
<--- Score

22. Does a troubleshooting guide exist or is it needed?
<--- Score

23. Is reporting being used or needed?
<--- Score

24. How do controls support value?
<--- Score

25. Do you monitor the Microsoft Office 365 decisions made and fine tune them as they evolve?
<--- Score

26. How will the process owner verify improvement in present and future sigma levels, process capabilities?
<--- Score

27. Is there a Microsoft Office 365 Communication plan covering who needs to get what information when?
<--- Score

28. What do you measure to verify effectiveness gains?
<--- Score

29. How do you encourage people to take control and responsibility?
<--- Score

30. Will any special training be provided for results interpretation?
<--- Score

31. Who controls what and who reports to whom?
<--- Score

32. Is new knowledge gained imbedded in the response plan?
<--- Score

33. How do you select, collect, align, and integrate Microsoft Office 365 data and information for tracking daily operations and overall organizational performance, including progress relative to strategic objectives and action plans?
<--- Score

34. Against what alternative is success being measured?
<--- Score

35. What other systems, operations, processes, and infrastructures (hiring practices, staffing, training, incentives/rewards, metrics/dashboards/scorecards, etc.) need updates, additions, changes, or deletions in order to facilitate knowledge transfer and improvements?
<--- Score

36. What do you stand for--and what are you against?
<--- Score

37. How do you plan on providing proper recognition and disclosure of supporting companies?
<--- Score

38. How do you establish and deploy modified action plans if circumstances require a shift in plans and

rapid execution of new plans?

<--- Score

39. How do your controls stack up?

<--- Score

40. Is there documentation that will support the successful operation of the improvement?

<--- Score

41. How might the organization capture best practices and lessons learned so as to leverage improvements across the business?

<--- Score

42. Who is the Microsoft Office 365 process owner?

<--- Score

43. What are the known security controls?

<--- Score

44. How will report readings be checked to effectively monitor performance?

<--- Score

45. What is the best design framework for Microsoft Office 365 organization now that, in a post industrial-age if the top-down, command and control model is no longer relevant?

<--- Score

46. Are the planned controls working?

<--- Score

47. How will new or emerging customer needs/requirements be checked/communicated to orient

the process toward meeting the new specifications and continually reducing variation?
<--- Score

48. How is change control managed?
<--- Score

49. How likely is the current Microsoft Office 365 plan to come in on schedule or on budget?
<--- Score

50. Where do ideas that reach policy makers and planners as proposals for Microsoft Office 365 strengthening and reform actually originate?
<--- Score

51. Are pertinent alerts monitored, analyzed and distributed to appropriate personnel?
<--- Score

52. Who controls critical resources?
<--- Score

53. Are the planned controls in place?
<--- Score

54. What quality tools were useful in the control phase?
<--- Score

55. Who has control over resources?
<--- Score

56. Are controls in place and consistently applied?
<--- Score

57. Are there documented procedures?
<--- Score

58. Who sets the Microsoft Office 365 standards?
<--- Score

59. Are new process steps, standards, and documentation ingrained into normal operations?
<--- Score

60. Do you monitor the effectiveness of your Microsoft Office 365 activities?
<--- Score

61. What adjustments to the strategies are needed?
<--- Score

62. You may have created your quality measures at a time when you lacked resources, technology wasn't up to the required standard, or low service levels were the industry norm. Have those circumstances changed?
<--- Score

63. Are you measuring, monitoring and predicting Microsoft Office 365 activities to optimize operations and profitability, and enhancing outcomes?
<--- Score

64. Does the response plan contain a definite closed loop continual improvement scheme (e.g., plan-do-check-act)?
<--- Score

65. Is knowledge gained on process shared and institutionalized?

<--- Score

66. Do the Microsoft Office 365 decisions you make today help people and the planet tomorrow?
<--- Score

67. Are documented procedures clear and easy to follow for the operators?
<--- Score

68. What are the critical parameters to watch?
<--- Score

69. Are suggested corrective/restorative actions indicated on the response plan for known causes to problems that might surface?
<--- Score

70. What can you control?
<--- Score

71. Is there a documented and implemented monitoring plan?
<--- Score

72. In the case of a Microsoft Office 365 project, the criteria for the audit derive from implementation objectives. an audit of a Microsoft Office 365 project involves assessing whether the recommendations outlined for implementation have been met. Can you track that any Microsoft Office 365 project is implemented as planned, and is it working?
<--- Score

73. What key inputs and outputs are being measured on an ongoing basis?

<--- Score

74. Will all users who access the email system on their company-owned mobile phones need to change their email settings in the phones to reflect the new email address?
<--- Score

75. Is there a standardized process?
<--- Score

76. How do senior leaders actions reflect a commitment to the organizations Microsoft Office 365 values?
<--- Score

77. What is the recommended frequency of auditing?
<--- Score

78. Can you adapt and adjust to changing Microsoft Office 365 situations?
<--- Score

79. Is there a recommended audit plan for routine surveillance inspections of Microsoft Office 365's gains?
<--- Score

80. What is the control/monitoring plan?
<--- Score

81. Implementation Planning: is a pilot needed to test the changes before a full roll out occurs?
<--- Score

82. Can support from partners be adjusted?

<--- Score

83. Is there a transfer of ownership and knowledge to process owner and process team tasked with the responsibilities.
<--- Score

84. What is your theory of human motivation, and how does your compensation plan fit with that view?
<--- Score

85. Have new or revised work instructions resulted?
<--- Score

86. What should you measure to verify efficiency gains?
<--- Score

87. What do your reports reflect?
<--- Score

88. Will the team be available to assist members in planning investigations?
<--- Score

Add up total points for this section:
_ _ _ _ _ = Total points for this section

Divided by: _ _ _ _ _ _ (number of statements answered) = _ _ _ _ _ _
Average score for this section

Transfer your score to the Microsoft Office 365 Index at the beginning of the Self-Assessment.

CRITERION #7: SUSTAIN:

INTENT: Retain the benefits.

In my belief, the answer to this question is clearly defined:

5 Strongly Agree

4 Agree

3 Neutral

2 Disagree

1 Strongly Disagree

1. How do you track customer value, profitability or financial return, organizational success, and sustainability?
<--- Score

2. Is there an option to participate only in the email portion of Office 365?
<--- Score

3. What stupid rule would you most like to kill?
<--- Score

4. How soon expected?
<--- Score

5. Ask yourself: how would you do this work if you only had one staff member to do it?
<--- Score

6. What should you stop doing?
<--- Score

7. If your company went out of business tomorrow, would anyone who doesn't get a paycheck here care?
<--- Score

8. How do you accomplish your long range Microsoft Office 365 goals?
<--- Score

9. Whose voice (department, ethnic group, women, older workers, etc) might you have missed hearing from in your company, and how might you amplify this voice to create positive momentum for your business?
<--- Score

10. How do you recover deleted mail items from Office 365?
<--- Score

11. Can you bring your personal device to work and use it with Office 365 ProPlus?
<--- Score

12. How do you manage Microsoft Office 365 Knowledge Management (KM)?

<--- Score

13. How do you proactively clarify deliverables and Microsoft Office 365 quality expectations?
<--- Score

14. What trouble can you get into?
<--- Score

15. What are the benefits of using Office 365 for email and calendaring?
<--- Score

16. Who will be responsible for deciding whether Microsoft Office 365 goes ahead or not after the initial investigations?
<--- Score

17. If you were responsible for initiating and implementing major changes in your organization, what steps might you take to ensure acceptance of those changes?
<--- Score

18. What are the success criteria that will indicate that Microsoft Office 365 objectives have been met and the benefits delivered?
<--- Score

19. How can I send an email out of a shared mailbox if is not migrated yet?
<--- Score

20. How do you lead with Microsoft Office 365 in mind?
<--- Score

21. What are the short and long-term Microsoft Office 365 goals?
<--- Score

22. How will information be used?
<--- Score

23. Are the assumptions believable and achievable?
<--- Score

24. Are you satisfied with your current role? If not, what is missing from it?
<--- Score

25. What is a feasible sequencing of reform initiatives over time?
<--- Score

26. If you do not follow, then how to lead?
<--- Score

27. When - over what timescale?
<--- Score

28. What is the approved browser version (Internet Explorer) Microsoft recommends?
<--- Score

29. What is the recommended frequency of auditing?
<--- Score

30. Are you paying enough attention to the partners your company depends on to succeed?
<--- Score

31. What is an unauthorized commitment?
<--- Score

32. Why is Microsoft Office 365 important for you now?
<--- Score

33. What unique value proposition (UVP) do you offer?
<--- Score

34. Are you using a design thinking approach and integrating Innovation, Microsoft Office 365 Experience, and Brand Value?
<--- Score

35. What relationships among Microsoft Office 365 trends do you perceive?
<--- Score

36. How do you set Microsoft Office 365 stretch targets and how do you get people to not only participate in setting these stretch targets but also that they strive to achieve these?
<--- Score

37. Do you have past Microsoft Office 365 successes?
<--- Score

38. What are the top 3 things at the forefront of your Microsoft Office 365 agendas for the next 3 years?
<--- Score

39. What other tools can achieve the same end?
<--- Score

40. Have benefits been optimized with all key

stakeholders?
<--- Score

41. Are there any activities that you can take off your to do list?
<--- Score

42. How do you foster innovation?
<--- Score

43. Why will customers want to buy your organizations products/services?
<--- Score

44. Who is the main stakeholder, with ultimate responsibility for driving Microsoft Office 365 forward?
<--- Score

45. How likely is it that a customer would recommend your company to a friend or colleague?
<--- Score

46. How do you compare alternatives?
<--- Score

47. Is there any reason to believe the opposite of my current belief?
<--- Score

48. What kind of crime could a potential new hire have committed that would not only not disqualify him/her from being hired by your organization, but would actually indicate that he/she might be a particularly good fit?
<--- Score

49. What management system can you use to leverage the Microsoft Office 365 experience, ideas, and concerns of the people closest to the work to be done?

<--- Score

50. Is maximizing Microsoft Office 365 protection the same as minimizing Microsoft Office 365 loss?

<--- Score

51. Does the vendor software enable collectors to easily log contact activity, providing an accurate, non-editable time stamp history?

<--- Score

52. Is a Microsoft Office 365 team work effort in place?

<--- Score

53. Can you break it down?

<--- Score

54. How much computer code does the company want to write?

<--- Score

55. How will migrating to Office 365 change things for me?

<--- Score

56. What did you miss in the interview for the worst hire you ever made?

<--- Score

57. Why a feasibility study?

<--- Score

58. What applications are included with Microsoft Office Pro Plus for Windows?
<--- Score

59. Can the available personnel provide the time?
<--- Score

60. Which individuals, teams or departments will be involved in Microsoft Office 365?
<--- Score

61. Is Microsoft Office 365 realistic, or are you setting yourself up for failure?
<--- Score

62. Who will maintain the system?
<--- Score

63. Who is on the team?
<--- Score

64. How can you become the company that would put you out of business?
<--- Score

65. How will Outlook .PST conversions be handled?
<--- Score

66. How long will it take to change?
<--- Score

67. Are assumptions made in Microsoft Office 365 stated explicitly?
<--- Score

68. Were lessons learned captured and communicated?
<--- Score

69. What is available in-house?
<--- Score

70. In a project to restructure Microsoft Office 365 outcomes, which stakeholders would you involve?
<--- Score

71. Political -is anyone trying to undermine this project?
<--- Score

72. Operational - will it work?
<--- Score

73. What is the craziest thing you can do?
<--- Score

74. How do you foster the skills, knowledge, talents, attributes, and characteristics you want to have?
<--- Score

75. Can an external user initiate an encrypted message to an internal user in Office 365?
<--- Score

76. Will all my current email be migrated to the new mailbox in Office 365?
<--- Score

77. Which functions and people interact with the supplier and or customer?
<--- Score

78. Can email be encrypted?

<--- Score

79. What does your signature ensure?

<--- Score

80. Have new benefits been realized?

<--- Score

81. Who else should you help?

<--- Score

82. Will there be any necessary staff changes (redundancies or new hires)?

<--- Score

83. What are the business goals Microsoft Office 365 is aiming to achieve?

<--- Score

84. What goals did you miss?

<--- Score

85. What are the expectations for using a modeling tool?

<--- Score

86. Marketing budgets are tighter, consumers are more skeptical, and social media has changed forever the way we talk about Microsoft Office 365. How do you gain traction?

<--- Score

87. Can the schedule be done in the given time?

<--- Score

88. What are the essentials of internal Microsoft Office 365 management?
<--- Score

89. How much contingency will be available in the budget?
<--- Score

90. Is there a set budget and/or secured funding for this project?
<--- Score

91. Are you changing as fast as the world around you?
<--- Score

92. How is implementation research currently incorporated into each of your goals?
<--- Score

93. How will licenses be managed?
<--- Score

94. How long will it take to get the technical expertise?
<--- Score

95. What must you excel at?
<--- Score

96. If I have access to a shared mailbox that hasnt been migrated yet, will I be able to access it?
<--- Score

97. How important is Microsoft Office 365 to the user organizations mission?

<--- Score

98. Why is it important to have senior management support for a Microsoft Office 365 project?
<--- Score

99. Will vaulted items be migrated to the new mailbox in Office 365?
<--- Score

100. Who will determine interim and final deadlines?
<--- Score

101. If you had to leave your organization for a year and the only communication you could have with employees/colleagues was a single paragraph, what would you write?
<--- Score

102. How will the new system be integrated?
<--- Score

103. What are the long-term Microsoft Office 365 goals?
<--- Score

104. What new services of functionality will be implemented next with Microsoft Office 365 ?
<--- Score

105. Are you maintaining a past–present–future perspective throughout the Microsoft Office 365 discussion?
<--- Score

106. Does the vendor have customers similar to

you?
<--- Score

107. How do you keep records, of what?
<--- Score

108. What are strategies for increasing support and reducing opposition?
<--- Score

109. What are the potential basics of Microsoft Office 365 fraud?
<--- Score

110. What would you recommend your friend do if he/she were facing this dilemma?
<--- Score

111. What are the main strengths of the current system?
<--- Score

112. What do we do when new problems arise?
<--- Score

113. How do you transition from the baseline to the target?
<--- Score

114. What are the key selling points of Google Apps vs Microsoft Office 365?
<--- Score

115. How easy/complex is the implementation?
<--- Score

116. What is the source of the strategies for Microsoft Office 365 strengthening and reform?
<--- Score

117. What Microsoft Office 365 skills are most important?
<--- Score

118. What you are going to do to affect the numbers?
<--- Score

119. What trophy do you want on your mantle?
<--- Score

120. What current systems have to be understood and/or changed?
<--- Score

121. How do you assess the Microsoft Office 365 pitfalls that are inherent in implementing it?
<--- Score

122. My name on my email address is wrong now. How can I get it changed?
<--- Score

123. Are there different kinds of service?
<--- Score

124. What hardware and software are available?
<--- Score

125. What are internal and external Microsoft Office 365 relations?
<--- Score

126. What is it like to work for you?
<--- Score

127. Can you deploy Office 365 ProPlus on shared public cloud environments?
<--- Score

128. How will you ensure you get what you expected?
<--- Score

129. How can you become more high-tech but still be high touch?
<--- Score

130. Will it be accepted by users?
<--- Score

131. Effectiveness of current resources and services?
<--- Score

132. What file attachment extensions are blocked?
<--- Score

133. How will security be handled and who will be responsible for what?
<--- Score

134. Is Microsoft Office 365 dependent on the successful delivery of a current project?
<--- Score

135. Do you see more potential in people than they do in themselves?
<--- Score

136. Are you relevant? Will you be relevant five years from now? Ten?
<--- Score

137. Will I still receive mail to my current email address – and for how long?
<--- Score

138. Why not do Microsoft Office 365?
<--- Score

139. If your customer were your grandmother, would you tell her to buy what you're selling?
<--- Score

140. Are upgrades free?
<--- Score

141. Can you deploy Office 365 ProPlus on Azure?
<--- Score

142. What one word do you want to own in the minds of your customers, employees, and partners?
<--- Score

143. Where can you break convention?
<--- Score

144. How do you ensure that implementations of Microsoft Office 365 products are done in a way that ensures safety?
<--- Score

145. What is your BATNA (best alternative to a negotiated agreement)?
<--- Score

146. What business benefits will Microsoft Office 365 goals deliver if achieved?

<--- Score

147. Do you currently possess the necessary technology?

<--- Score

148. What are major deficiencies of current system?

<--- Score

149. How do you create buy-in?

<--- Score

150. What is your formula for success in Microsoft Office 365 ?

<--- Score

151. What are the challenges?

<--- Score

152. Is the impact that Microsoft Office 365 has shown?

<--- Score

153. What is the range of capabilities?

<--- Score

154. What have you done to protect your business from competitive encroachment?

<--- Score

155. Would it be part of project Active Directory in sync with SharePoint?

<--- Score

156. What projects are going on in the organization today, and what resources are those projects using from the resource pools?
<--- Score

157. Does Office 365 come with an email archive (currently known as Enterprise Vault)?
<--- Score

158. What are the advantages & disadvantages?
<--- Score

159. Can the bottom line be quantified yet?
<--- Score

160. Who are your customers?
<--- Score

161. Are the criteria for selecting recommendations stated?
<--- Score

162. How is the information to be extracted?
<--- Score

163. Which Microsoft Office 365 goals are the most important?
<--- Score

164. What have been your experiences in defining long range Microsoft Office 365 goals?
<--- Score

165. Do you feel that more should be done in the

Microsoft Office 365 area?

<--- Score

166. What are your personal philosophies regarding Microsoft Office 365 and how do they influence your work?

<--- Score

167. Where is the information to be found?

<--- Score

168. What is effective Microsoft Office 365?

<--- Score

169. What may be the consequences for the performance of an organization if all stakeholders are not consulted regarding Microsoft Office 365?

<--- Score

170. How will the company pay for the application?

<--- Score

171. How does Microsoft Office 365 integrate with other business initiatives?

<--- Score

172. Do you have the right people on the bus?

<--- Score

173. Will the Outlook Web Access link change?

<--- Score

174. How do you deal with Microsoft Office 365 changes?

<--- Score

175. Who do we want your customers to become?
<--- Score

176. Can you deploy Office 365 ProPlus media to your personal device to work from home?
<--- Score

177. How do you stay inspired?
<--- Score

178. Are your responses positive or negative?
<--- Score

179. Where will the application run?
<--- Score

180. Are there any disadvantages to implementing Microsoft Office 365? There might be some that are less obvious?
<--- Score

181. Who will manage the integration of tools?
<--- Score

182. How do you listen to customers to obtain actionable information?
<--- Score

183. Which devices can be used to access Office deployment on a network server?
<--- Score

184. When information truly is ubiquitous, when reach and connectivity are completely global, when computing resources are infinite, and when a whole

new set of impossibilities are not only possible, but happening, what will that do to your business?
<--- Score

185. What will be the consequences to the stakeholder (financial, reputation etc) if Microsoft Office 365 does not go ahead or fails to deliver the objectives?
<--- Score

186. Does Office 365 allow customers to be HIPAA/ HITECH Act compliant?
<--- Score

187. Can you maintain your growth without detracting from the factors that have contributed to your success?
<--- Score

188. What would the stakeholders like to achieve?
<--- Score

189. Web-based or Installed?
<--- Score

190. Are you / should you be revolutionary or evolutionary?
<--- Score

191. Think of your Microsoft Office 365 project, what are the main functions?
<--- Score

192. How many machines can be activated via shared computer activation?
<--- Score

193. How do you determine the key elements that affect Microsoft Office 365 workforce satisfaction, how are these elements determined for different workforce groups and segments?
<--- Score

194. What is your competitive advantage?
<--- Score

195. Would you rather sell to knowledgeable and informed customers or to uninformed customers?
<--- Score

196. What to study and conclude?
<--- Score

197. What is the funding source for this project?
<--- Score

198. What are you trying to prove to yourself, and how might it be hijacking your life and business success?
<--- Score

199. Who do you think the world wants your organization to be?
<--- Score

200. Why should you adopt a Microsoft Office 365 framework?
<--- Score

201. Do you say no to customers for no reason?
<--- Score

202. How do you decide how much to remunerate an

employee?

<--- Score

203. What is the purpose of Microsoft Office 365 in relation to the mission?

<--- Score

204. Which Office 365 subscriptions include shared computer activation?

<--- Score

205. What is the size limitation for attachments?

<--- Score

206. How does Microsoft handle your security and privacy?

<--- Score

207. How soon will the benefits accrue?

<--- Score

208. Do you think Microsoft Office 365 accomplishes the goals you expect it to accomplish?

<--- Score

209. What are the usability implications of Microsoft Office 365 actions?

<--- Score

210. Do you have an implicit bias for capital investments over people investments?

<--- Score

211. What is something you believe that nearly no one agrees with you on?

<--- Score

212. What is wrong with the present situation?
<--- Score

213. Will My Email Address Be Changing?
<--- Score

214. To whom do you add value?
<--- Score

215. How much does Microsoft Office 365 help?
<--- Score

216. What are specific Microsoft Office 365 rules to follow?
<--- Score

217. How will you know that the Microsoft Office 365 project has been successful?
<--- Score

218. Why do and why don't your customers like your organization?
<--- Score

219. Has implementation been effective in reaching specified objectives so far?
<--- Score

220. How do you make it meaningful in connecting Microsoft Office 365 with what users do day-to-day?
<--- Score

221. What are you challenging?
<--- Score

222. How can I access a shared resource that is not migrated yet?
<--- Score

223. Is your basic point _____ or _____?
<--- Score

224. Is it economical; do you have the time and money?
<--- Score

225. Do you have enough freaky customers in your portfolio pushing you to the limit day in and day out?
<--- Score

226. Are current services reliable?
<--- Score

227. What is the estimated value of the project?
<--- Score

228. What training is available to help you?
<--- Score

229. What are the rules and assumptions your industry operates under? What if the opposite were true?
<--- Score

230. What would have to be true for the option on the table to be the best possible choice?
<--- Score

231. What information is critical to your organization that your executives are ignoring?
<--- Score

232. Do you know what you are doing? And who do you call if you don't?
<--- Score

233. Who will use the information?
<--- Score

234. Who is responsible for Microsoft Office 365?
<--- Score

235. Is staff properly trained to fully utilize features?
<--- Score

236. Which models, tools and techniques are necessary?
<--- Score

237. What are your most important goals for the strategic Microsoft Office 365 objectives?
<--- Score

238. What was the last experiment you ran?
<--- Score

239. If the project overruns, what are the consequences?
<--- Score

240. Who do you want your customers to become?
<--- Score

241. Whom among your colleagues do you trust, and for what?
<--- Score

242. What are the gaps in your knowledge and experience?
<--- Score

243. Are new benefits received and understood?
<--- Score

244. How do customers see your organization?
<--- Score

245. What are current Microsoft Office 365 paradigms?
<--- Score

246. Who, on the executive team or the board, has spoken to a customer recently?
<--- Score

247. What should the new system be able to do?
<--- Score

248. Is the Microsoft Office 365 organization completing tasks effectively and efficiently?
<--- Score

249. How do you reset your office 365 password?
<--- Score

250. What role does communication play in the success or failure of a Microsoft Office 365 project?
<--- Score

251. If you weren't already in this business, would you enter it today? And if not, what are you going to do about it?
<--- Score

252. Will all our distribution lists and Shared Mailboxes automatically change to the new format?

<--- Score

253. Hardware (what to buy, buy/lease)?

<--- Score

254. Mobility increases as Office 365 can be used on 5 devices including Smartphones and Tablets How do you access your Office 365 e-mail via the web?

<--- Score

255. Who are the key stakeholders?

<--- Score

256. What knowledge, skills and characteristics mark a good Microsoft Office 365 project manager?

<--- Score

257. What is the size of your mailbox in Office 365?

<--- Score

258. Do you have the right capabilities and capacities?

<--- Score

259. Can you install and use Office 365 ProPlus with your Mac device?

<--- Score

260. Who benefits?

<--- Score

261. Do you think you know, or do you know you know ?

<--- Score

262. How do you know if you are successful?
<--- Score

263. If no one would ever find out about your accomplishments, how would you lead differently?
<--- Score

264. How will you insure seamless interoperability of Microsoft Office 365 moving forward?
<--- Score

265. What is the kind of project structure that would be appropriate for your Microsoft Office 365 project, should it be formal and complex, or can it be less formal and relatively simple?
<--- Score

266. How will the benefits accrue?
<--- Score

267. What happens at your organization when people fail?
<--- Score

268. How do you go about securing Microsoft Office 365?
<--- Score

269. How can you incorporate support to ensure safe and effective use of Microsoft Office 365 into the services that you provide?
<--- Score

270. What happens if you do not have enough

funding?

<--- Score

271. What browsers can you use to access the Office 365 on the web?

<--- Score

272. Will this include my calendar entries, contacts, and tasks?

<--- Score

273. Are all key stakeholders present at all Structured Walkthroughs?

<--- Score

274. Where will the application originate?

<--- Score

275. What happens when a new employee joins the organization?

<--- Score

276. What threat is Microsoft Office 365 addressing?

<--- Score

277. Who have you, as a company, historically been when you've been at your best?

<--- Score

278. Is there a work around that you can use?

<--- Score

279. Who is responsible for ensuring appropriate resources (time, people and money) are allocated to Microsoft Office 365?

<--- Score

280. How do you provide a safe environment -physically and emotionally?
<--- Score

281. Which alternative is the best investment?
<--- Score

282. What the maximum allowed attachment size for your message?
<--- Score

283. In the past year, what have you done (or could you have done) to increase the accurate perception of your company/brand as ethical and honest?
<--- Score

284. For staff that use Microsoft Office on a limited basis, including sharing workstations, what is the best option for them?
<--- Score

285. Make or Buy?
<--- Score

286. How can you negotiate Microsoft Office 365 successfully with a stubborn boss, an irate client, or a deceitful coworker?
<--- Score

287. What are the barriers to increased Microsoft Office 365 production?
<--- Score

288. What files/records are in use?
<--- Score

289. At what moment would you think; Will I get fired?
<--- Score

290. If there were zero limitations, what would you do differently?
<--- Score

291. How do you cross-sell and up-sell your Microsoft Office 365 success?
<--- Score

292. Do Microsoft Office 365 rules make a reasonable demand on a users capabilities?
<--- Score

293. What Microsoft Office 365 modifications can you make work for you?
<--- Score

294. What is your question? Why?
<--- Score

295. How do you govern and fulfill your societal responsibilities?
<--- Score

296. Will Office be identical on a PC, a Mac, and a mobile device?
<--- Score

297. If you got fired and a new hire took your place, what would she do different?
<--- Score

298. How do you select software tools?

<--- Score

299. Who will provide the final approval of Microsoft Office 365 deliverables?
<--- Score

300. Is current throughput and response time adequate?
<--- Score

301. Who is responsible for errors?
<--- Score

302. Are you making progress, and are you making progress as Microsoft Office 365 leaders?
<--- Score

303. Will I still have access to the same distribution lists?
<--- Score

304. How are you doing compared to your industry?
<--- Score

305. Who uses your product in ways you never expected?
<--- Score

306. What are the mailbox sizes?
<--- Score

307. How is antivirus/anti-malware handled?
<--- Score

308. What are the differences between the online Office applications and the fully installed Office

applications?

<--- Score

309. Can you do all this work?

<--- Score

310. How do you keep the momentum going?

<--- Score

311. How will you motivate the stakeholders with the least vested interest?

<--- Score

312. Who should the new system serve?

<--- Score

313. In retrospect, of the projects that you pulled the plug on, what percent do you wish had been allowed to keep going, and what percent do you wish had ended earlier?

<--- Score

314. Instead of going to current contacts for new ideas, what if you reconnected with dormant contacts--the people you used to know? If you were going reactivate a dormant tie, who would it be?

<--- Score

315. How long should the new system last (useful life)?

<--- Score

316. Who are four people whose careers you have enhanced?

<--- Score

317. Did your employees make progress today?
<--- Score

318. Why should people listen to you?
<--- Score

319. How do you engage the workforce, in addition to satisfying them?
<--- Score

320. What are the key enablers to make this Microsoft Office 365 move?
<--- Score

321. What are the real constraints on project deadlines?
<--- Score

322. What potential megatrends could make your business model obsolete?
<--- Score

323. Will partners still be able to act as site owners?
<--- Score

324. What counts that you are not counting?
<--- Score

325. What is the competition/comparable unit doing?
<--- Score

326. What type of information is desired?
<--- Score

327. How do you maintain Microsoft Office 365's Integrity?
<--- Score

Add up total points for this section:
_ _ _ _ _ = Total points for this section

Divided by: _ _ _ _ _ _ (number of statements answered) = _ _ _ _ _ _
Average score for this section

Transfer your score to the Microsoft Office 365 Index at the beginning of the Self-Assessment.

Microsoft Office 365 and Managing Projects, Criteria for Project Managers:

1.0 Initiating Process Group: Microsoft Office 365

1. Professionals want to know what is expected from them what are the deliverables?

2. Are you certain deliverables are properly completed and meet quality standards?

3. Are there resources to maintain and support the outcome of the Microsoft Office 365 project?

4. If the risk event occurs, what will you do?

5. How will it affect me?

6. Will the Microsoft Office 365 project meet the client requirements, and will it achieve the business success criteria that justified doing the Microsoft Office 365 project in the first place?

7. Were resources available as planned?

8. How should needs be met?

9. What are the inputs required to produce the deliverables?

10. At which cmmi level are software processes documented, standardized, and integrated into a standard to-be practiced process for your organization?

11. First of all, should any action be taken?

12. If action is called for, what form should it take?

13. How do you help others satisfy needs?

14. Who is involved in each phase?

15. Information sharing?

16. Contingency planning. if a risk event occurs, what will you do?

17. During which stage of Risk planning are risks prioritized based on probability and impact?

18. What are the tools and techniques to be used in each phase?

19. How well did you do?

20. Mitigate. what will you do to minimize the impact should the risk event occur?

1.1 Project Charter: Microsoft Office 365

21. How do you manage integration?

22. What are the assigned resources?

23. What are some examples of a business case?

24. Assumptions and constraints: what assumptions were made in defining the Microsoft Office 365 project?

25. When is a charter needed?

26. When do you use a Microsoft Office 365 project Charter?

27. If finished, on what date did it finish?

28. Why the improvements?

29. Major high-level milestone targets: what events measure progress?

30. What material?

31. How high should you set your goals?

32. Fit with other Products Compliments – Cannibalizes?

33. Why Outsource?

34. How much?

35. Will this replace an existing product?

36. What is the most common tool for helping define the detail?

37. What metrics could you look at?

38. Market – identify products market, including whether it is outside of the objective: what is the purpose of the program or Microsoft Office 365 project?

39. Why use a Microsoft Office 365 project charter?

40. Whose input and support will this Microsoft Office 365 project require?

1.2 Stakeholder Register: Microsoft Office 365

41. What opportunities exist to provide communications?

42. Is your organization ready for change?

43. How big is the gap?

44. What is the power of the stakeholder?

45. How will reports be created?

46. Who wants to talk about Security?

47. What are the major Microsoft Office 365 project milestones requiring communications or providing communications opportunities?

48. How should employers make voices heard?

49. What & Why?

50. How much influence do they have on the Microsoft Office 365 project?

51. Who are the stakeholders?

52. Who is managing stakeholder engagement?

1.3 Stakeholder Analysis Matrix: Microsoft Office 365

53. Geographical, export, import?

54. Who holds positions of responsibility in interested organizations?

55. What tools would help you communicate?

56. Disadvantages of proposition?

57. Financial reserves, likely returns?

58. Is changing technology threatening your organizations position?

59. Which conditions out of the control of the management are crucial for the achievement of the immediate objective?

60. Do the stakeholders goals and expectations support or conflict with the Microsoft Office 365 project goals?

61. Alliances: with which other actors is the actor allied, how are they interconnected?

62. What do people from other organizations see as your strengths?

63. Competitors vulnerabilities?

64. Competitor intentions - various?

65. What is in it for you?

66. Industry or lifestyle trends?

67. What could your organization improve?

68. Why do you need to manage Microsoft Office 365 project Risk?

69. How do they affect the Microsoft Office 365 project and its outcomes?

70. Identify the stakeholders levels most frequently used –or at least sought– in your Microsoft Office 365 projects and for which purpose?

71. Supporters; who are the supporters?

72. Price, value, quality?

2.0 Planning Process Group: Microsoft Office 365

73. Did the program design/ implementation strategy adequately address the planning stage necessary to set up structures, hire staff etc.?

74. To what extent have the target population and participants made the activities own, taking an active role in it?

75. How many days can task X be late in starting without affecting the Microsoft Office 365 project completion date?

76. You are creating your WBS and find that you keep decomposing tasks into smaller and smaller units. How can you tell when you are done?

77. Why is it important to determine activity sequencing on Microsoft Office 365 projects?

78. In what ways can the governance of the Microsoft Office 365 project be improved so that it has greater likelihood of achieving future sustainability?

79. How does activity resource estimation affect activity duration estimation?

80. What factors are contributing to progress or delay in the achievement of products and results?

81. Are the necessary foundations in place to ensure

the sustainability of the results of the Microsoft Office 365 project?

82. If a risk event occurs, what will you do?

83. What will you do to minimize the impact should a risk event occur?

84. In what way has the Microsoft Office 365 project come up with innovative measures for problem-solving?

85. How can you tell when you are done?

86. Just how important is your work to the overall success of the Microsoft Office 365 project?

87. How will it affect you?

88. What good practices or successful experiences or transferable examples have been identified?

89. What is the critical path for this Microsoft Office 365 project, and what is the duration of the critical path?

90. You did your readings, yes?

91. To what extent have public/private national resources and/or counterparts been mobilized to contribute to the programs objective and produce results and impacts?

92. Does the program have follow-up mechanisms (to verify the quality of the products, punctuality of delivery, etc.) to measure progress in the achievement

of the envisaged results?

2.1 Project Management Plan: Microsoft Office 365

93. What are the constraints?

94. Are there any client staffing expectations?

95. What are the training needs?

96. What should you drop in order to add something new?

97. What are the deliverables?

98. Is mitigation authorized or recommended?

99. What are the assumptions?

100. Does the selected plan protect privacy?

101. How do you manage time?

102. What happened during the process that you found interesting?

103. Who is the sponsor?

104. Is the appropriate plan selected based on your organizations objectives and evaluation criteria expressed in Principles and Guidelines policies?

105. What is the justification?

106. What is the business need?

107. What would you do differently what did not work?

108. What is Microsoft Office 365 project scope management?

109. Was the peer (technical) review of the cost estimates duly coordinated with the cost estimate center of expertise and addressed in the review documentation and certification?

110. What if, for example, the positive direction and vision of your organization causes expected trends to change resulting in greater need than expected?

111. Is there an incremental analysis/cost effectiveness analysis of proposed mitigation features based on an approved method and using an accepted model?

2.2 Scope Management Plan: Microsoft Office 365

112. Has a sponsor been identified?

113. Have all team members been part of identifying risks?

114. Are measurements and feedback mechanisms incorporated in tracking work effort & refining work estimating techniques?

115. Staffing Requirements?

116. Have activity relationships and interdependencies within tasks been adequately identified?

117. Is there a formal set of procedures supporting Issues Management?

118. What is the unique product, service or result?

119. Are funding resource estimates sufficiently detailed and documented for use in planning and tracking the Microsoft Office 365 project?

120. Is documentation created for communication with the suppliers and Vendors?

121. Are corrective actions taken when actual results are substantially different from detailed Microsoft Office 365 project plan (variances)?

122. Knowing the health of the Microsoft Office 365 project – What is the status?

123. Are changes in scope (deliverable commitments) agreed to by all affected groups & individuals?

124. What do you need to do to accomplish the goal or goals?

125. Have the personnel with the necessary skills and competence been identified and has agreement for participation in the Microsoft Office 365 project been reached with the appropriate management?

126. Has appropriate allowance been made for the effect of the learning curve on all personnel joining the Microsoft Office 365 project who do not have the required prior industry, functional & technical expertise?

127. Are any non-compliance issues that exist due to organizations practices?

128. Do you have the reasons why the changes to your organizational systems and capabilities are required?

129. What is the estimated cost of creating and implementing?

130. What are the risks that could significantly affect the schedule of the Microsoft Office 365 project?

131. Have all documents been archived in a Microsoft Office 365 project repository for each release?

2.3 Requirements Management Plan: Microsoft Office 365

132. How will the requirements become prioritized?

133. Is there formal agreement on who has authority to approve a change in requirements?

134. Will you document changes to requirements?

135. Will you have access to stakeholders when you need them?

136. Is stakeholder risk tolerance an important factor for the requirements process in this Microsoft Office 365 project?

137. Who will approve the requirements (and if multiple approvers, in what order)?

138. Is the change control process documented?

139. Business analysis scope?

140. Who will perform the analysis?

141. Does the Microsoft Office 365 project have a Change Control process?

142. How will unresolved questions be handled once approval has been obtained?

143. If it exists, where is it housed?

144. Has the requirements team been instructed in the Change Control process?

145. Is infrastructure setup part of your Microsoft Office 365 project?

146. Do you have price sheets and a methodology for determining the total proposal cost?

147. Who will finally present the work or product(s) for acceptance?

148. Will you use tracing to help understand the impact of a change in requirements?

149. Is requirements work dependent on any other specific Microsoft Office 365 project or non-Microsoft Office 365 project activities (e.g. funding, approvals, procurement)?

150. Define the help desk model. who will take full responsibility?

151. To see if a requirement statement is sufficiently well-defined, read it from the developers perspective. Mentally add the phrase, call me when youre done to the end of the requirement and see if that makes you nervous. In other words, would you need additional clarification from the author to understand the requirement well enough to design and implement it?

2.4 Requirements Documentation: Microsoft Office 365

152. How can you document system requirements?

153. What are the attributes of a customer?

154. Do your constraints stand?

155. Basic work/business process; high-level, what is being touched?

156. How much testing do you need to do to prove that your system is safe?

157. Are there legal issues?

158. Is the origin of the requirement clearly stated?

159. What happens when requirements are wrong?

160. What can tools do for us?

161. What facilities must be supported by the system?

162. How much does requirements engineering cost?

163. Completeness. are all functions required by the customer included?

164. Can the requirement be changed without a large impact on other requirements?

165. What is your Elevator Speech?

166. Is new technology needed?

167. Has requirements gathering uncovered information that would necessitate changes?

168. Can you check system requirements?

169. Who provides requirements?

170. Where do you define what is a customer, what are the attributes of customer?

171. What images does it conjure?

2.5 Requirements Traceability Matrix: Microsoft Office 365

172. What percentage of Microsoft Office 365 projects are producing traceability matrices between requirements and other work products?

173. Describe the process for approving requirements so they can be added to the traceability matrix and Microsoft Office 365 project work can be performed. Will the Microsoft Office 365 project requirements become approved in writing?

174. Will you use a Requirements Traceability Matrix?

175. Is there a requirements traceability process in place?

176. What is the WBS?

177. Do you have a clear understanding of all subcontracts in place?

178. Why do you manage scope?

179. How small is small enough?

180. How do you manage scope?

181. Why use a WBS?

182. How will it affect the stakeholders personally in their career?

183. What are the chronologies, contingencies, consequences, criteria?

2.6 Project Scope Statement: Microsoft Office 365

184. Is an issue management process documented and filed?

185. Were key Microsoft Office 365 project stakeholders brought into the Microsoft Office 365 project Plan?

186. Elements that deal with providing the detail?

187. Is there a baseline plan against which to measure progress?

188. Has the Microsoft Office 365 project scope statement been reviewed as part of the baseline process?

189. Is there a process (test plans, inspections, reviews) defined for verifying outputs for each task?

190. Who will you recommend approve the change, and when do you recommend the change reviews occur?

191. What are the possible consequences should a risk come to occur?

192. Are the meetings set up to have assigned note takers that will add action/issues to the issue list?

193. Is the Microsoft Office 365 project organization

documented and on file?

194. Will the Microsoft Office 365 project risks be managed according to the Microsoft Office 365 projects risk management process?

195. Will all Microsoft Office 365 project issues be unconditionally tracked through the issue resolution process?

196. Relevant - ask yourself can you get there; why are you doing this Microsoft Office 365 project?

197. Have you been able to thoroughly document the Microsoft Office 365 projects assumptions and constraints?

198. What is change?

199. Are there completion/verification criteria defined for each task producing an output?

200. Has the format for tracking and monitoring schedules and costs been defined?

201. Where and how does the team fit within your organization structure?

202. Elements of scope management that deal with concept development ?

2.7 Assumption and Constraint Log: Microsoft Office 365

203. What to do at recovery?

204. What weaknesses do you have?

205. Are there standards for code development?

206. Is the amount of effort justified by the anticipated value of forming a new process?

207. Should factors be unpredictable over time?

208. After observing execution of process, is it in compliance with the documented Plan?

209. Are there ways to reduce the time it takes to get something approved?

210. How do you design an auditing system?

211. Does the plan conform to standards?

212. Have adequate resources been provided by management to ensure Microsoft Office 365 project success?

213. What do you audit?

214. Are there processes in place to ensure that all the terms and code concepts have been documented consistently?

215. Has a Microsoft Office 365 project Communications Plan been developed?

216. Diagrams and tables are included to account for complex concepts and increase overall readability?

217. Are there procedures in place to effectively manage interdependencies with other Microsoft Office 365 projects / systems?

218. What other teams / processes would be impacted by changes to the current process, and how?

219. Are processes for release management of new development from coding and unit testing, to integration testing, to training, and production defined and followed?

220. Does a specific action and/or state that is known to violate security policy occur?

221. What does an audit system look like?

222. Are there processes in place to ensure internal consistency between the source code components?

2.8 Work Breakdown Structure: Microsoft Office 365

223. How will you and your Microsoft Office 365 project team define the Microsoft Office 365 projects scope and work breakdown structure?

224. Do you need another level?

225. When would you develop a Work Breakdown Structure?

226. How much detail?

227. Is the work breakdown structure (wbs) defined and is the scope of the Microsoft Office 365 project clear with assigned deliverable owners?

228. How far down?

229. Why is it useful?

230. When does it have to be done?

231. Where does it take place?

232. What is the probability of completing the Microsoft Office 365 project in less that xx days?

233. Can you make it?

234. When do you stop?

235. How many levels?

236. Is it still viable?

237. What has to be done?

238. What is the probability that the Microsoft Office 365 project duration will exceed xx weeks?

239. Is it a change in scope?

240. Who has to do it?

241. How big is a work-package?

242. Why would you develop a Work Breakdown Structure?

2.9 WBS Dictionary: Microsoft Office 365

243. Does the contractor have procedures which permit identification of recurring or non-recurring costs as necessary?

244. Are retroactive changes to budgets for completed work specifically prohibited in an established procedure, and is this procedure adhered to?

245. Does the contractors system provide unit or lot costs when applicable?

246. Are the overhead pools formally and adequately identified?

247. What went right?

248. Do work packages reflect the actual way in which the work will be done and are they meaningful products or management-oriented subdivisions of a higher level element of work?

249. Incurrence of actual indirect costs in excess of budgets, by element of expense?

250. Are significant decision points, constraints, and interfaces identified as key milestones?

251. Are detailed work packages planned as far in advance as practicable?

252. Are records maintained to show how undistributed budgets are controlled?

253. Are work packages assigned to performing organizations?

254. Are retroactive changes to BCWS and BCWP prohibited except for correction of errors or for normal accounting adjustments?

255. Is each control account assigned to a single organizational element directly responsible for the work and identifiable to a single element of the CWBS?

256. Are estimates of costs at completion generated in a rational, consistent manner?

257. The wbs is developed as part of a joint planning session. and how do you know that youhave done this right?

258. Do work packages consist of discrete tasks which are adequately described?

259. Does the contractors system provide for determination of price variance by comparing planned Vs actual commitments?

260. Are the bases and rates for allocating costs from each indirect pool consistently applied?

2.10 Schedule Management Plan: Microsoft Office 365

261. Is the development plan and/or process documented?

262. Cost / benefit analysis?

263. Is a process defined to measure the performance of the schedule management process itself?

264. Are corrective actions and variances reported?

265. Is there an approved case?

266. Has the budget been baselined?

267. Are the schedule estimates reasonable given the Microsoft Office 365 project?

268. Have all involved Microsoft Office 365 project stakeholders and work groups committed to the Microsoft Office 365 project?

269. Have all documents been archived in a Microsoft Office 365 project repository for each release?

270. Where is the scheduling tool and who has access to it to view it?

271. Has the scope management document been updated and distributed to help prevent scope creep?

272. Is the critical path valid?

273. Does the business case include how the Microsoft Office 365 project aligns with your organizations strategic goals & objectives?

274. Have Microsoft Office 365 project success criteria been defined?

275. Are the processes for schedule assessment and analysis defined?

276. Are software metrics formally captured, analyzed and used as a basis for other Microsoft Office 365 project estimates?

277. Are the activity durations realistic and at an appropriate level of detail for effective management?

278. Pareto diagrams, statistical sampling, flow charting or trend analysis used quality monitoring?

279. Are all key components of a Quality Assurance Plan present?

280. Does the Microsoft Office 365 project have a Statement of Work?

2.11 Activity List: Microsoft Office 365

281. Can you determine the activity that must finish, before this activity can start?

282. What will be performed?

283. What is your organizations history in doing similar activities?

284. What did not go as well?

285. What went well?

286. When do the individual activities need to start and finish?

287. How should ongoing costs be monitored to try to keep the Microsoft Office 365 project within budget?

288. What are the critical bottleneck activities?

289. What went wrong?

290. What is the LF and LS for each activity?

291. Should you include sub-activities?

292. Where will it be performed?

293. How much slack is available in the Microsoft Office 365 project?

294. How do you determine the late start (LS) for each

activity?

295. How will it be performed?

296. Is infrastructure setup part of your Microsoft Office 365 project?

297. Is there anything planned that does not need to be here?

298. How can the Microsoft Office 365 project be displayed graphically to better visualize the activities?

299. When will the work be performed?

2.12 Activity Attributes: Microsoft Office 365

300. Resource is assigned to?

301. Activity: what is Missing?

302. Activity: what is In the Bag?

303. Which method produces the more accurate cost assignment?

304. What activity do you think you should spend the most time on?

305. Were there other ways you could have organized the data to achieve similar results?

306. Have you identified the Activity Leveling Priority code value on each activity?

307. Where else does it apply?

308. Time for overtime?

309. Would you consider either of corresponding activities an outlier?

310. What is the general pattern here?

311. How many resources do you need to complete the work scope within a limit of X number of days?

312. Why?

313. How much activity detail is required?

314. Are the required resources available or need to be acquired?

315. Do you feel very comfortable with your prediction?

316. Can you re-assign any activities to another resource to resolve an over-allocation?

317. What is missing?

2.13 Milestone List: Microsoft Office 365

318. How soon can the activity finish?

319. What is the market for your technology, product or service?

320. Competitive advantages?

321. New USPs?

322. Timescales, deadlines and pressures?

323. Own known vulnerabilities?

324. What specific improvements did you make to the Microsoft Office 365 project proposal since the previous time?

325. Environmental effects?

326. What date will the task finish?

327. Gaps in capabilities?

328. How late can the activity start?

329. Usps (unique selling points)?

330. How will you get the word out to customers?

331. Vital contracts and partners?

332. Political effects?

333. Milestone pages should display the UserID of the person who added the milestone. Does a report or query exist that provides this audit information?

334. What has been done so far?

335. Which path is the critical path?

2.14 Network Diagram: Microsoft Office 365

336. What can be done concurrently?

337. Where do you schedule uncertainty time?

338. Why must you schedule milestones, such as reviews, throughout the Microsoft Office 365 project?

339. What job or jobs follow it?

340. How difficult will it be to do specific activities on this Microsoft Office 365 project?

341. What activity must be completed immediately before this activity can start?

342. Will crashing x weeks return more in benefits than it costs?

343. Where do schedules come from?

344. What must be completed before an activity can be started?

345. Are the required resources available?

346. What controls the start and finish of a job?

347. Are the gantt chart and/or network diagram updated periodically and used to assess the overall Microsoft Office 365 project timetable?

348. What activities must occur simultaneously with this activity?

349. Review the logical flow of the network diagram. Take a look at which activities you have first and then sequence the activities. Do they make sense?

350. Which type of network diagram allows you to depict four types of dependencies?

351. What are the Major Administrative Issues?

352. What are the tools?

353. If a current contract exists, can you provide the vendor name, contract start, and contract expiration date?

354. What to do and When?

355. If x is long, what would be the completion time if you break x into two parallel parts of y weeks and z weeks?

2.15 Activity Resource Requirements: Microsoft Office 365

356. What are constraints that you might find during the Human Resource Planning process?

357. How many signatures do you require on a check and does this match what is in your policy and procedures?

358. Why do you do that?

359. When does monitoring begin?

360. What is the Work Plan Standard?

361. How do you handle petty cash?

362. Are there unresolved issues that need to be addressed?

363. Other support in specific areas?

364. Do you use tools like decomposition and rolling-wave planning to produce the activity list and other outputs?

365. Anything else?

366. Organizational Applicability?

367. Which logical relationship does the PDM use most often?

2.16 Resource Breakdown Structure: Microsoft Office 365

368. Who will be used as a Microsoft Office 365 project team member?

369. Which resource planning tool provides information on resource responsibility and accountability?

370. The list could probably go on, but, the thing that you would most like to know is, How long & How much?

371. Who will use the system?

372. What is the primary purpose of the human resource plan?

373. Which resources should be in the resource pool?

374. Is predictive resource analysis being done?

375. What defines a successful Microsoft Office 365 project?

376. Goals for the Microsoft Office 365 project. What is each stakeholders desired outcome for the Microsoft Office 365 project?

377. What is each stakeholders desired outcome for the Microsoft Office 365 project?

378. Who needs what information?

379. How should the information be delivered?

380. What can you do to improve productivity?

381. Who delivers the information?

382. How difficult will it be to do specific activities on this Microsoft Office 365 project?

383. What is the purpose of assigning and documenting responsibility?

384. Why do you do it?

385. What are the requirements for resource data?

2.17 Activity Duration Estimates: Microsoft Office 365

386. Did anything besides luck make a difference between success and failure?

387. Is earned value analysis completed to assess Microsoft Office 365 project performance?

388. Which best describes how this affects the Microsoft Office 365 project?

389. Is the work performed reviewed against contractual objectives?

390. Which is the BEST thing to do to try to complete a Microsoft Office 365 project two days earlier?

391. What are the key components of a Microsoft Office 365 project communications plan?

392. Briefly summarize the work done by Maslow, Herzberg, McClellan, McGregor, Ouchi, Thamhain and Wilemon, and Covey. How do theories relate to Microsoft Office 365 project management?

393. Which suggestions do you find most useful?

394. List five reasons why organizations outsource. Why is there a growing trend in outsourcing, especially in the government?

395. After changes are approved are Microsoft Office

365 project documents updated and distributed?

396. How does poking fun at technical professionals communications skills impact the industry and educational programs?

397. How does Microsoft Office 365 project management relate to other disciplines?

398. What are the nine areas of expertise?

399. If Microsoft Office 365 project time and cost are not as important as the number of resources used each month, which is the BEST thing to do?

400. What Microsoft Office 365 project was the first to use modern Microsoft Office 365 project management?

401. Is a provider selected based upon defined evaluation criteria?

402. What is the difference between using brainstorming and the Delphi technique for risk identification?

403. Which is the BEST Microsoft Office 365 project management tool to use to determine the longest time the Microsoft Office 365 project will take?

404. Why is it important to determine activity sequencing on Microsoft Office 365 projects?

2.18 Duration Estimating Worksheet: Microsoft Office 365

405. What info is needed?

406. Why estimate time and cost?

407. Is the Microsoft Office 365 project responsive to community need?

408. Done before proceeding with this activity or what can be done concurrently?

409. How should ongoing costs be monitored to try to keep the Microsoft Office 365 project within budget?

410. When does your organization expect to be able to complete it?

411. What work will be included in the Microsoft Office 365 project?

412. What is your role?

413. What is next?

414. For other activities, how much delay can be tolerated?

415. Can the Microsoft Office 365 project be constructed as planned?

416. What is the total time required to complete the

Microsoft Office 365 project if no delays occur?

417. Define the work as completely as possible. What work will be included in the Microsoft Office 365 project?

418. Value pocket identification & quantification what are value pockets?

419. Is a construction detail attached (to aid in explanation)?

420. Will the Microsoft Office 365 project collaborate with the local community and leverage resources?

421. Does the Microsoft Office 365 project provide innovative ways for stakeholders to overcome obstacles or deliver better outcomes?

422. Small or large Microsoft Office 365 project?

2.19 Project Schedule: Microsoft Office 365

423. How can you address that situation?

424. Verify that the update is accurate. Are all remaining durations correct?

425. What is risk management?

426. If there are any qualifying green components to this Microsoft Office 365 project, what portion of the total Microsoft Office 365 project cost is green?

427. How can you minimize or control changes to Microsoft Office 365 project schedules?

428. What is Microsoft Office 365 project management?

429. Why or why not?

430. Change management required?

431. What is risk?

432. Understand the constraints used in preparing the schedule. Are activities connected because logic dictates the order in which others occur?

433. Are there activities that came from a template or previous Microsoft Office 365 project that are not applicable on this phase of this Microsoft Office 365

project?

434. It allows the Microsoft Office 365 project to be delivered on schedule. How Do you Use Schedules?

435. What is the purpose of a Microsoft Office 365 project schedule?

436. Activity charts and bar charts are graphical representations of a Microsoft Office 365 project schedule ...how do they differ?

437. How does a Microsoft Office 365 project get to be a year late ?

438. Are procedures defined by which the Microsoft Office 365 project schedule may be changed?

439. Is infrastructure setup part of your Microsoft Office 365 project?

440. Are you working on the right risks?

441. How do you know that youhave done this right?

442. Why do you think schedule issues often cause the most conflicts on Microsoft Office 365 projects?

2.20 Cost Management Plan: Microsoft Office 365

443. Is the assigned Microsoft Office 365 project manager a PMP (Certified Microsoft Office 365 project manager) and experienced?

444. Is there general agreement & acceptance of the current status and progress of the Microsoft Office 365 project?

445. If you sold 10x widgets on a day, what would the affect on costs be?

446. Is a pmo (Microsoft Office 365 project management office) in place and provide oversight to the Microsoft Office 365 project?

447. What does this mean to a cost or scheduler manager?

448. Weve met your goals?

449. Are trade-offs between accepting the risk and mitigating the risk identified?

450. Are issues raised, assessed, actioned, and resolved in a timely and efficient manner?

451. What would the life cycle costs be?

452. What is your organizations history in doing similar tasks?

453. Contingency rundown curve be used on the Microsoft Office 365 project?

454. How relevant is this attribute to this Microsoft Office 365 project or audit?

455. Are assumptions being identified, recorded, analyzed, qualified and closed?

456. Are the payment terms being followed?

457. Does the detailed work plan match the complexity of tasks with the capabilities of personnel?

458. Time management – how will the schedule impact of changes be estimated and approved?

459. Cost estimate preparation – What cost estimates will be prepared during the Microsoft Office 365 project phases?

460. Owner, contractor, and subcontractors?

2.21 Activity Cost Estimates: Microsoft Office 365

461. If you are asked to lower your estimate because the price is too high, what are your options?

462. What were things that you did very well and want to do the same again on the next Microsoft Office 365 project?

463. Were sponsors and decision makers available when needed outside regularly scheduled meetings?

464. How do you manage cost?

465. How difficult will it be to do specific tasks on the Microsoft Office 365 project?

466. Does the activity use a common approach or business function to deliver its results?

467. What is the activity inventory?

468. Are cost subtotals needed?

469. What areas does the group agree are the biggest success on the Microsoft Office 365 project?

470. Why do you manage cost?

471. Who determines the quality and expertise of contractors?

472. Can you change your activities?

473. Certification of actual expenditures?

474. What is procurement?

475. How Award?

476. When do you enter into PPM?

477. What is the last item a Microsoft Office 365 project manager must do to finalize Microsoft Office 365 project close-out?

478. Would you hire them again?

479. Padding is bad and contingencies are good. what is the difference?

480. What communication items need improvement?

2.22 Cost Estimating Worksheet: Microsoft Office 365

481. What will others want?

482. What can be included?

483. What is the purpose of estimating?

484. What is the estimated labor cost today based upon this information?

485. Ask: are others positioned to know, are others credible, and will others cooperate?

486. Does the Microsoft Office 365 project provide innovative ways for stakeholders to overcome obstacles or deliver better outcomes?

487. Will the Microsoft Office 365 project collaborate with the local community and leverage resources?

488. Who is best positioned to know and assist in identifying corresponding factors?

489. Can a trend be established from historical performance data on the selected measure and are the criteria for using trend analysis or forecasting methods met?

490. Is the Microsoft Office 365 project responsive to community need?

491. What costs are to be estimated?

492. What additional Microsoft Office 365 project(s) could be initiated as a result of this Microsoft Office 365 project?

493. How will the results be shared and to whom?

494. Identify the timeframe necessary to monitor progress and collect data to determine how the selected measure has changed?

495. What happens to any remaining funds not used?

496. Is it feasible to establish a control group arrangement?

2.23 Cost Baseline: Microsoft Office 365

497. How will cost estimates be used?

498. What do you want to measure ?

499. Has the Microsoft Office 365 projected annual cost to operate and maintain the product(s) or service(s) been approved and funded?

500. How concrete were original objectives?

501. Verify business objectives. Are others appropriate, and well-articulated?

502. Are there contingencies or conditions related to the acceptance?

503. Eac -estimate at completion, what is the total job expected to cost?

504. Have the lessons learned been filed with the Microsoft Office 365 project Management Office?

505. What is the reality?

506. How fast?

507. Should a more thorough impact analysis be conducted?

508. Have all the product or service deliverables been

accepted by the customer?

509. On budget?

510. What deliverables come first?

511. What does a good WBS NOT look like?

512. Will the Microsoft Office 365 project fail if the change request is not executed?

513. Does the suggested change request seem to represent a necessary enhancement to the product?

514. What is cost and Microsoft Office 365 project cost management?

2.24 Quality Management Plan: Microsoft Office 365

515. How does your organization maintain a safe and healthy work environment?

516. How are corresponding standards measured?

517. Have all involved stakeholders and work groups committed to the Microsoft Office 365 project?

518. Is there a Quality Management Plan?

519. How does training support what is important to your organization and the individual?

520. How is staff trained on the recording of field notes?

521. Account for the procedures used to verify the data quality of the data being reviewed?

522. Do the data quality objectives communicate the intended program need?

523. Who needs a qmp?

524. How does your organization ensure the quality, reliability, and user-friendliness of its hardware and software?

525. What changes can you make that will result in improvement?

526. Have you eliminated all duplicative tasks or manual efforts, where appropriate?

527. Can it be done better?

528. How does your organization measure customer satisfaction/dissatisfaction?

529. Does the program conduct field testing?

530. Are there trends or hot spots?

531. How do senior leaders create and communicate values and performance expectations?

532. How do your action plans support the strategic objectives?

533. How do you decide what information to record?

2.25 Quality Metrics: Microsoft Office 365

534. How does one achieve stability?

535. What group is empowered to define quality requirements?

536. If the defect rate during testing is substantially higher than that of the previous release (or a similar product), then ask: Did you plan for and actually improve testing effectiveness?

537. What metrics do you measure?

538. What are your organizations expectations for its quality Microsoft Office 365 project?

539. Was review conducted per standard protocols?

540. Was material distributed on time?

541. Are applicable standards referenced and available?

542. Have alternatives been defined in the event that failure occurs?

543. What forces exist that would cause them to change?

544. When will the Final Guidance will be issued?

545. Are documents on hand to provide explanations of privacy and confidentiality?

546. How effective are your security tests?

547. What is the timeline to meet your goal?

548. How are requirements conflicts resolved?

549. What are you trying to accomplish?

550. What do you measure?

551. Was the overall quality better or worse than previous products?

552. Which data do others need in one place to target areas of improvement?

553. Is there a set of procedures to capture, analyze and act on quality metrics?

2.26 Process Improvement Plan: Microsoft Office 365

554. Have the supporting tools been developed or acquired?

555. What actions are needed to address the problems and achieve the goals?

556. Has a process guide to collect the data been developed?

557. Where do you focus?

558. What lessons have you learned so far?

559. Who should prepare the process improvement action plan?

560. Purpose of goal: the motive is determined by asking, why do you want to achieve this goal?

561. Everyone agrees on what process improvement is, right?

562. Are there forms and procedures to collect and record the data?

563. What is the return on investment?

564. Have the frequency of collection and the points in the process where measurements will be made been determined?

565. Why do you want to achieve the goal?

566. Are you meeting the quality standards?

567. Where are you now?

568. What personnel are the champions for the initiative?

569. What is the test-cycle concept?

570. Does explicit definition of the measures exist?

571. Where do you want to be?

572. Are you following the quality standards?

573. Why quality management?

2.27 Responsibility Assignment Matrix: Microsoft Office 365

574. What are some important Microsoft Office 365 project communications management tools?

575. Are records maintained to show how management reserves are used?

576. Changes in the current direct and Microsoft Office 365 projected base?

577. Contemplated overhead expenditure for each period based on the best information currently available?

578. Evaluate the performance of operating organizations?

579. Changes in the nature of the overhead requirements?

580. Are indirect costs accumulated for comparison with the corresponding budgets?

581. Who is responsible for work and budgets for each wbs?

582. What expertise is not available in your department?

583. Budgets assigned to major functional organizations?

584. Do you know how your people are allocated?

585. How do you manage remotely to staff in other Divisions?

586. What is the number one predictor of a groups productivity?

587. Who is going to do that work?

588. Are management actions taken to reduce indirect costs when there are significant adverse variances?

589. What travel needed?

2.28 Roles and Responsibilities: Microsoft Office 365

590. What is working well?

591. Once the responsibilities are defined for the Microsoft Office 365 project, have the deliverables, roles and responsibilities been clearly communicated to every participant?

592. What is working well within your organizations performance management system?

593. Are governance roles and responsibilities documented?

594. Do you take the time to clearly define roles and responsibilities on Microsoft Office 365 project tasks?

595. What should you do now to ensure that you are meeting all expectations of your current position?

596. What expectations were NOT met?

597. Implementation of actions: Who are the responsible units?

598. What specific behaviors did you observe?

599. What areas would you highlight for changes or improvements?

600. What are your major roles and responsibilities

in the area of performance measurement and assessment?

601. Are Microsoft Office 365 project team roles and responsibilities identified and documented?

602. Is there a training program in place for stakeholders covering expectations, roles and responsibilities and any addition knowledge others need to be good stakeholders?

603. What should you do now to ensure that you are exceeding expectations and excelling in your current position?

604. What expectations were met?

605. How well did the Microsoft Office 365 project Team understand the expectations of specific roles and responsibilities?

606. What areas of supervision are challenging for you?

607. Does your vision/mission support a culture of quality data?

608. Once the responsibilities are defined for the Microsoft Office 365 project, have the deliverables, roles and responsibilities been clearly communicated to every participant?

609. Concern: where are you limited or have no authority, where you can not influence?

2.29 Human Resource Management Plan: Microsoft Office 365

610. What were things that you need to improve?

611. Are changes in deliverable commitments agreed to by all affected groups & individuals?

612. Are change requests logged and managed?

613. Is the steering committee active in Microsoft Office 365 project oversight?

614. What were things that you did well, and could improve, and how?

615. Are Microsoft Office 365 project team members committed fulltime?

616. Are tasks tracked by hours?

617. Are milestone deliverables effectively tracked and compared to Microsoft Office 365 project plan?

618. Are software metrics formally captured, analyzed and used as a basis for other Microsoft Office 365 project estimates?

619. Are meeting minutes captured and sent out after the meeting?

620. Are mitigation strategies identified?

621. Have all unresolved risks been documented?

622. Are internal Microsoft Office 365 project status meetings held at reasonable intervals?

623. Are the Microsoft Office 365 project plans updated on a frequent basis?

624. Are the people assigned to the Microsoft Office 365 project sufficiently qualified?

625. Do all stakeholders know how to access this repository and where to find the Microsoft Office 365 project documentation?

626. What did you have to assume to be true to complete the charter?

627. How to convince employees that this is a necessary process?

2.30 Communications Management Plan: Microsoft Office 365

628. Is the stakeholder role recognized by your organization?

629. Will messages be directly related to the release strategy or phases of the Microsoft Office 365 project?

630. Can you think of other people who might have concerns or interests?

631. Timing: when do the effects of the communication take place?

632. Are there potential barriers between the team and the stakeholder?

633. In your work, how much time is spent on stakeholder identification?

634. Do you prepare stakeholder engagement plans?

635. What is the political influence?

636. What is the stakeholders level of authority?

637. Are the stakeholders getting the information others need, are others consulted, are concerns addressed?

638. Who have you worked with in past, similar initiatives?

639. Which team member will work with each stakeholder?

640. Do you then often overlook a key stakeholder or stakeholder group?

641. Are others part of the communications management plan?

642. What approaches to you feel are the best ones to use?

643. Do you feel a register helps?

644. Why is stakeholder engagement important?

645. How did the term stakeholder originate?

646. Do you have members of your team responsible for certain stakeholders?

647. What does the stakeholder need from the team?

2.31 Risk Management Plan: Microsoft Office 365

648. What risks are tracked?

649. Risk probability and impact: how will the probabilities and impacts of risk items be assessed?

650. Is security a central objective?

651. Are people attending meetings and doing work?

652. What would you do?

653. Are staff committed for the duration of the product?

654. Technology risk: is the Microsoft Office 365 project technically feasible?

655. Who/what can assist?

656. Was an original risk assessment/risk management plan completed?

657. Market risk -will the new service or product be useful to your organization or marketable to others?

658. Has something like this been done before?

659. What are some questions that should be addressed in a risk management plan?

660. Are the best people available?

661. Where are you confronted with risks during the business phases?

662. Are tool mentors available?

663. What are the cost, schedule and resource impacts of avoiding the risk?

664. What risks are necessary to achieve success?

665. What other risks are created by choosing an avoidance strategy?

666. How will the Microsoft Office 365 project know if your organizations risk response actions were effective?

2.32 Risk Register: Microsoft Office 365

667. When would you develop a risk register?

668. Severity Prediction?

669. What are the assumptions and current status that support the assessment of the risk?

670. What is the appropriate level of risk management for this Microsoft Office 365 project?

671. When is it going to be done?

672. What is a Risk?

673. User involvement: do you have the right users?

674. Why would you develop a risk register?

675. What risks might negatively or positively affect achieving the Microsoft Office 365 project objectives?

676. What has changed since the last period?

677. Technology risk -is the Microsoft Office 365 project technically feasible?

678. Budget and schedule: what are the estimated costs and schedules for performing risk-related activities?

679. Risk documentation: what reporting formats and processes will be used for risk management activities?

680. What is your current and future risk profile?

681. Manageability – have mitigations to the risk been identified?

682. What is a Community Risk Register?

683. How is a Community Risk Register created?

2.33 Probability and Impact Assessment: Microsoft Office 365

684. What is the likelihood?

685. What are the likely future requirements?

686. Do end-users have realistic expectations?

687. Risks should be identified during which phase of Microsoft Office 365 project management life cycle?

688. Risk may be made during which step of risk management?

689. Is the customer willing to commit significant time to the requirements gathering process?

690. Are testing tools available and suitable?

691. What new technologies are being explored in the same area?

692. Is it necessary to deeply assess all Microsoft Office 365 project risks?

693. Mitigation -how can you avoid the risk?

694. What will be cost of redeployment of personnel?

695. Do you have a mechanism for managing change?

696. Is the present organizational structure for

handling the Microsoft Office 365 project sufficient?

697. Are staff committed for the duration of the Microsoft Office 365 project?

698. Can it be enlarged by drawing people from other areas of your organization?

699. How is risk handled within this Microsoft Office 365 project organization?

700. Is the customer technically sophisticated in the product area?

701. Do requirements put excessive performance constraints on the product?

702. To what extent is the chosen technology maturing?

703. Are the facilities, expertise, resources, and management know-how available to handle the situation?

2.34 Probability and Impact Matrix: Microsoft Office 365

704. Are the software tools integrated with each other?

705. Why do you need to manage Microsoft Office 365 project Risk?

706. What is the level of commitment and professionalism?

707. What will be cost of redeployment of the personnel?

708. What will be the environmental impact of the Microsoft Office 365 project?

709. Do the requirements require the creation of new algorithms?

710. Is the customer willing to establish rapid communication links with the developer?

711. What should be done NEXT?

712. Which should be probably done NEXT?

713. What are its business ethics?

714. Are you on schedule?

715. What will be the likely political environment

during the life of the Microsoft Office 365 project?

716. What will the damage be?

717. What risks were tracked?

718. What are the risks involved in appointing external agencies to manage the Microsoft Office 365 project?

719. What are the methods to deal with risks?

2.35 Risk Data Sheet: Microsoft Office 365

720. What is the environment within which you operate (social trends, economic, community values, broad based participation, national directions etc.)?

721. What was measured?

722. Who has a vested interest in how you perform as your organization (our stakeholders)?

723. What if client refuses?

724. How reliable is the data source?

725. What actions can be taken to eliminate or remove risk?

726. How do you handle product safely?

727. What do people affected think about the need for, and practicality of preventive measures?

728. What are the main opportunities available to you that you should grab while you can?

729. Is the data sufficiently specified in terms of the type of failure being analyzed, and its frequency or probability?

730. What is the duration of infection (the length of time the host is infected with the organizm) in a

normal healthy human host?

731. Do effective diagnostic tests exist?

732. Will revised controls lead to tolerable risk levels?

733. What will be the consequences if it happens?

734. During work activities could hazards exist?

735. If it happens, what are the consequences?

736. What can happen?

737. What are you trying to achieve (Objectives)?

738. What is the chance that it will happen?

739. What were the Causes that contributed?

2.36 Procurement Management Plan: Microsoft Office 365

740. Does the Microsoft Office 365 project have a formal Microsoft Office 365 project Charter?

741. How and when do you enter into Microsoft Office 365 project Procurement Management?

742. Have adequate resources been provided by management to ensure Microsoft Office 365 project success?

743. Are software metrics formally captured, analyzed and used as a basis for other Microsoft Office 365 project estimates?

744. Do Microsoft Office 365 project teams & team members report on status / activities / progress?

745. Is there a Steering Committee in place?

746. Are parking lot items captured?

747. Are internal Microsoft Office 365 project status meetings held at reasonable intervals?

748. Are cause and effect determined for risks when others occur?

749. Alignment to strategic goals & objectives?

750. Are Microsoft Office 365 project leaders

committed to this Microsoft Office 365 project full time?

751. Has the Microsoft Office 365 project manager been identified?

752. Sensitivity analysis?

753. Has a capability assessment been conducted?

754. Have Microsoft Office 365 project management standards and procedures been identified / established and documented?

2.37 Source Selection Criteria: Microsoft Office 365

755. What will you use to capture evaluation and subsequent documentation?

756. When is it appropriate to issue a Draft Request for Proposal (DRFP)?

757. What can not be disclosed?

758. What are the most critical evaluation criteria that prove to be tiebreakers in the evaluation of proposals?

759. How should oral presentations be prepared for?

760. Are there any common areas of weaknesses or deficiencies in the proposals in the competitive range?

761. What past performance information should be requested?

762. What is price analysis and when should it be performed?

763. What should be considered when developing evaluation standards?

764. What are the most common types of rating systems?

765. Do you have a plan to document consensus

results including disposition of any disagreement by individual evaluators?

766. Is this a cost contract?

767. How do you ensure an integrated assessment of proposals?

768. What does an evaluation address and what does a sample resemble?

769. Are considerations anticipated?

770. What should a Draft Request for Proposal (DRFP) include?

771. How are clarifications and communications appropriately used?

772. What is the basis of an estimate and what assumptions were made?

773. How are oral presentations documented?

774. Are they compliant with all technical requirements?

2.38 Stakeholder Management Plan: Microsoft Office 365

775. Is the schedule updated on a periodic basis?

776. Have Microsoft Office 365 project success criteria been defined?

777. Are non-critical path items updated and agreed upon with the teams?

778. Why would you develop a Microsoft Office 365 project Business Plan?

779. Have all stakeholders been identified?

780. What procedures will be utilised to ensure effective monitoring of Microsoft Office 365 project progress?

781. Are schedule deliverables actually delivered?

782. Is staff trained on the software technologies that are being used on the Microsoft Office 365 project?

783. Has a structured approach been used to break work effort into manageable components (WBS)?

784. Where does the information come from?

785. What are the criteria for selecting other suppliers, including subcontractors?

786. What is to be the method of release?

787. Is the steering committee active in Microsoft Office 365 project oversight?

788. Have the procedures for identifying budget variances been followed?

789. Are Microsoft Office 365 project contact logs kept up to date?

790. What would you gain if you spent time working to improve this process?

791. Have stakeholder accountabilities & responsibilities been clearly defined?

2.39 Change Management Plan: Microsoft Office 365

792. Who will fund the training?

793. How prevalent is Resistance to Change?

794. What risks may occur upfront, during implementation and after implementation?

795. What processes are in place to manage knowledge about the Microsoft Office 365 project?

796. What is the most cynical response it can receive?

797. What risks may occur upfront?

798. How do you know the requirements you documented are the right ones?

799. Has the training provider been established?

800. What prerequisite knowledge or training is required?

801. Where will the funds come from?

802. Has the training co-ordinator been provided with the training details and put in place the necessary arrangements?

803. Will all field readiness criteria have been practically met prior to training roll-out?

804. Is there a software application relevant to this deliverable?

805. What would be an estimate of the total cost for the activities required to carry out the change initiative?

806. What prerequisite knowledge do corresponding groups need?

807. What goal(s) do you hope to accomplish?

808. Who is responsible for which tasks?

809. Change invariability confront many relationships especially the already stated that require a set of behaviours What roles with in your organization are affected and how?

810. What skills, education, knowledge, or work experiences should the resources have for each identified competency?

811. Has this been negotiated with the customer and sponsor?

3.0 Executing Process Group: Microsoft Office 365

812. What are the key components of the Microsoft Office 365 project communications plan?

813. What are crucial elements of successful Microsoft Office 365 project plan execution?

814. How will you know you did it?

815. What are the typical Microsoft Office 365 project management skills?

816. Just how important is your work to the overall success of the Microsoft Office 365 project?

817. Do the partners have sufficient financial capacity to keep up the benefits produced by the programme?

818. How does Microsoft Office 365 project management relate to other disciplines?

819. How is Microsoft Office 365 project performance information created and distributed?

820. How will professionals learn what is expected from them what the deliverables are?

821. What is the shortest possible time it will take to complete this Microsoft Office 365 project?

822. What are the critical steps involved with strategy

mapping?

823. Is the Microsoft Office 365 project making progress in helping to achieve the set results?

824. How can software assist in procuring goods and services?

825. How could you control progress of your Microsoft Office 365 project?

826. Are decisions made in a timely manner?

827. Does the case present a realistic scenario?

828. Have operating capacities been created and/or reinforced in partners?

829. Why do you need a good WBS to use Microsoft Office 365 project management software?

3.1 Team Member Status Report: Microsoft Office 365

830. Why is it to be done?

831. Is there evidence that staff is taking a more professional approach toward management of your organizations Microsoft Office 365 projects?

832. How does this product, good, or service meet the needs of the Microsoft Office 365 project and your organization as a whole?

833. Are the products of your organizations Microsoft Office 365 projects meeting customers objectives?

834. Does your organization have the means (staff, money, contract, etc.) to produce or to acquire the product, good, or service?

835. How much risk is involved?

836. How will resource planning be done?

837. Do you have an Enterprise Microsoft Office 365 project Management Office (EPMO)?

838. Are your organizations Microsoft Office 365 projects more successful over time?

839. What specific interest groups do you have in place?

840. How can you make it practical?

841. How it is to be done?

842. The problem with Reward & Recognition Programs is that the truly deserving people all too often get left out. How can you make it practical?

843. What is to be done?

844. Does the product, good, or service already exist within your organization?

845. Will the staff do training or is that done by a third party?

846. Does every department have to have a Microsoft Office 365 project Manager on staff?

847. When a teams productivity and success depend on collaboration and the efficient flow of information, what generally fails them?

848. Are the attitudes of staff regarding Microsoft Office 365 project work improving?

3.2 Change Request: Microsoft Office 365

849. Has your address changed?

850. How fast will change requests be approved?

851. Will all change requests and current status be logged?

852. What is a Change Request Form?

853. Since there are no change requests in your Microsoft Office 365 project at this point, what must you have before you begin?

854. What are the duties of the change control team?

855. Will there be a change request form in use?

856. Has the change been highlighted and documented in the CSCI?

857. How can you ensure that changes have been made properly?

858. When to submit a change request?

859. Screen shots or attachments included in a Change Request?

860. Who will perform the change?

861. Can static requirements change attributes like the size of the change be used to predict reliability in execution?

862. Should staff call into the helpdesk or go to the website?

863. Who is included in the change control team?

864. Will the change use memory to the extent that other functions will be not have sufficient memory to operate effectively?

865. How is the change documented (format, content, storage)?

866. Are there requirements attributes that are strongly related to the occurrence of defects and failures?

867. How is quality being addressed on the Microsoft Office 365 project?

868. Will all change requests be unconditionally tracked through this process?

3.3 Change Log: Microsoft Office 365

869. Is this a mandatory replacement?

870. How does this relate to the standards developed for specific business processes?

871. Will the Microsoft Office 365 project fail if the change request is not executed?

872. Does the suggested change request represent a desired enhancement to the products functionality?

873. Is the submitted change a new change or a modification of a previously approved change?

874. Is the change backward compatible without limitations?

875. How does this change affect the timeline of the schedule?

876. Where do changes come from?

877. Is the requested change request a result of changes in other Microsoft Office 365 project(s)?

878. Is the change request open, closed or pending?

879. When was the request approved?

880. Is the change request within Microsoft Office 365 project scope?

881. When was the request submitted?

882. Do the described changes impact on the integrity or security of the system?

883. Who initiated the change request?

884. How does this change affect scope?

3.4 Decision Log: Microsoft Office 365

885. What are the cost implications?

886. Is your opponent open to a non-traditional workflow, or will it likely challenge anything you do?

887. At what point in time does loss become unacceptable?

888. What is the line where eDiscovery ends and document review begins?

889. How does provision of information, both in terms of content and presentation, influence acceptance of alternative strategies?

890. How effective is maintaining the log at facilitating organizational learning?

891. How do you know when you are achieving it?

892. What is the average size of your matters in an applicable measurement?

893. Is everything working as expected?

894. Which variables make a critical difference?

895. Behaviors; what are guidelines that the team has identified that will assist them with getting the most out of team meetings?

896. What is your overall strategy for quality control /

quality assurance procedures?

897. It becomes critical to track and periodically revisit both operational effectiveness; Are you noticing all that you need to, and are you interpreting what you see effectively?

898. Meeting purpose; why does this team meet?

899. What alternatives/risks were considered?

900. Do strategies and tactics aimed at less than full control reduce the costs of management or simply shift the cost burden?

901. What eDiscovery problem or issue did your organization set out to fix or make better?

902. How consolidated and comprehensive a story can you tell by capturing currently available incident data in a central location and through a log of key decisions during an incident?

903. What makes you different or better than others companies selling the same thing?

904. How does an increasing emphasis on cost containment influence the strategies and tactics used?

3.5 Quality Audit: Microsoft Office 365

905. How does your organization know that its management system is appropriately effective and constructive?

906. How does your organization know that the range and quality of its social and recreational services and facilities are appropriately effective and constructive in meeting the needs of staff?

907. How does your organization know that its planning processes are appropriately effective and constructive?

908. How does the organization know that its system for maintaining and advancing the capabilities of its staff, particularly in relation to the Mission of the organization, is appropriately effective and constructive?

909. How does your organization know that the support for its staff is appropriately effective and constructive?

910. How does your organization know that it is appropriately effective and constructive in preparing its staff for organizational aspirations?

911. How does your organization know that its research planning and management systems are appropriately effective and constructive in enabling quality research outcomes?

912. How does your organization know that it provides a safe and healthy environment?

913. How does your organization know that its staffing profile is optimally aligned with the capability requirements implicit (or explicit) in its Strategic Plan?

914. Do the suppliers use a formal quality system?

915. Are complaint files maintained?

916. How does your organization know that its Mission, Vision and Values Statements are appropriate and effectively guiding your organization?

917. How does your organization know that its methods are appropriately effective and constructive?

918. How does your organization know that the range and quality of its accommodation, catering and transportation services are appropriately effective and constructive?

919. How does your organization know that its research programs are appropriately effective and constructive?

920. Does the suppliers quality system have a written procedure for corrective action when a defect occurs?

921. Has a written procedure been established to identify devices during all stages of receipt, reconditioning, distribution and installation so that mix-ups are prevented?

922. Are all complaints involving the possible failure

of a device, labeling, or packaging to meet any of its specifications reviewed, evaluated, and investigated?

923. Are storage areas and reconditioning operations designed to prevent mix-ups and assure orderly handling of both the distressed and reconditioned devices?

924. How does your organization know that its system for recruiting the best staff possible are appropriately effective and constructive?

3.6 Team Directory: Microsoft Office 365

925. What needs to be communicated?

926. How will you accomplish and manage the objectives?

927. Process decisions: do job conditions warrant additional actions to collect job information and document on-site activity?

928. Process decisions: how well was task order work performed?

929. Who will be the stakeholders on your next Microsoft Office 365 project?

930. Process decisions: are there any statutory or regulatory issues relevant to the timely execution of work?

931. How will the team handle changes?

932. When will you produce deliverables?

933. Decisions: what could be done better to improve the quality of the constructed product?

934. Where should the information be distributed?

935. How and in what format should information be presented?

936. Contract requirements complied with?

937. Timing: when do the effects of communication take place?

938. How does the team resolve conflicts and ensure tasks are completed?

939. Who are the Team Members?

940. Process decisions: do invoice amounts match accepted work in place?

941. Who will write the meeting minutes and distribute?

942. What are you going to deliver or accomplish?

943. Process decisions: are contractors adequately prosecuting the work?

3.7 Team Operating Agreement: Microsoft Office 365

944. Did you determine the technology methods that best match the messages to be communicated?

945. What types of accommodations will be formulated and put in place for sustaining the team?

946. Do team members reside in more than two countries?

947. Have you established procedures that team members can follow to work effectively together, such as a team operating agreement?

948. What are the safety issues/risks that need to be addressed and/or that the team needs to consider?

949. How will your group handle planned absences?

950. How will you resolve conflict efficiently and respectfully?

951. Are there differences in access to communication and collaboration technology based on team member location?

952. Are there the right people on your team?

953. Must your team members rely on the expertise of other members to complete tasks?

954. The method to be used in the decision making process; Will it be consensus, majority rule, or the supervisor having the final say?

955. Are there influences outside the team that may affect performance, and if so, have you identified and addressed them?

956. Do you upload presentation materials in advance and test the technology?

957. Do you send out the agenda and meeting materials in advance?

958. Do you post meeting notes and the recording (if used) and notify participants?

959. Do you leverage technology engagement tools group chat, polls, screen sharing, etc.?

960. What administrative supports will be put in place to support the team and the teams supervisor?

961. Do you prevent individuals from dominating the meeting?

962. Are there more than two functional areas represented by your team?

963. Did you draft the meeting agenda?

3.8 Team Performance Assessment: Microsoft Office 365

964. To what degree can all members engage in open and interactive considerations?

965. To what degree can team members vigorously define the teams purpose in considerations with others who are not part of the functioning team?

966. To what degree do the goals specify concrete team work products?

967. To what degree are staff involved as partners in the improvement process?

968. To what degree can team members meet frequently enough to accomplish the teams ends?

969. What do you think is the most constructive thing that could be done now to resolve considerations and disputes about method variance?

970. To what degree are the relative importance and priority of the goals clear to all team members?

971. Which situations call for a more extreme type of adaptiveness in which team members actually re-define roles?

972. Does more radicalness mean more perceived benefits?

973. To what degree are the teams goals and objectives clear, simple, and measurable?

974. To what degree does the teams purpose contain themes that are particularly meaningful and memorable?

975. What are you doing specifically to develop the leaders around you?

976. To what degree do team members articulate the teams work approach?

977. When does the medium matter?

978. How hard do you try to make a good selection?

979. How do you keep key people outside the group informed about its accomplishments?

980. Do friends perform better than acquaintances?

981. To what degree will the approach capitalize on and enhance the skills of all team members in a manner that takes into consideration other demands on members of the team?

982. Delaying market entry: how long is too long?

983. What is method variance?

3.9 Team Member Performance Assessment: Microsoft Office 365

984. Who they are?

985. What are the evaluation strategies (e.g., reaction, learning, behavior, results) used. What evaluation results did you have?

986. How are evaluation results utilized?

987. What variables that affect team members achievement are within your control?

988. What steps have you taken to improve performance?

989. How do you know that all team members are learning?

990. How is the timing of assessments organized (e.g., pre/post-test, single point during training, multiple reassessment during training)?

991. How do you start collaborating?

992. How do you use data to inform instruction and improve staff achievement?

993. How accurately is your plan implemented?

994. What are acceptable governance changes?

995. Who is responsible?

996. Is it critical or vital to the job?

997. How effective is training that is delivered through technology-based platforms?

998. What changes do you need to make to align practices with beliefs?

999. Why were corresponding selected?

1000. To what extent did the evaluation influence the instructional path, such as with adaptive testing?

1001. What entity leads the process, selects a potential restructuring option and develops the plan?

1002. How should adaptive assessments be implemented?

3.10 Issue Log: Microsoft Office 365

1003. In classifying stakeholders, which approach to do so are you using?

1004. Are the stakeholders getting the information they need, are they consulted, are concerns addressed?

1005. What is a change?

1006. Why multiple evaluators?

1007. What is the stakeholders political influence?

1008. What effort will a change need?

1009. Are they needed?

1010. Is there an important stakeholder who is actively opposed and will not receive messages?

1011. Why not more evaluators?

1012. What approaches do you use?

1013. What are the stakeholders interrelationships?

1014. What is a Stakeholder?

1015. How do you manage communications?

1016. Is the issue log kept in a safe place?

1017. What is the status of the issue?

4.0 Monitoring and Controlling Process Group: Microsoft Office 365

1018. Propriety: who needs to be involved in the evaluation to be ethical?

1019. Are there areas that need improvement?

1020. How well did the chosen processes fit the needs of the Microsoft Office 365 project?

1021. Based on your Microsoft Office 365 project communication management plan, what worked well?

1022. How were collaborations developed, and how are they sustained?

1023. What is the timeline for the Microsoft Office 365 project?

1024. Did it work?

1025. Who are the Microsoft Office 365 project stakeholders?

1026. Specific - is the objective clear in terms of what, how, when, and where the situation will be changed?

1027. Do the products created live up to the necessary quality?

1028. What resources are necessary?

1029. Are the necessary foundations in place to ensure the sustainability of the results of the programme?

1030. What business situation is being addressed?

1031. What resources (both financial and non-financial) are available/needed?

1032. What areas were overlooked on this Microsoft Office 365 project?

1033. Is there undesirable impact on staff or resources?

1034. How many potential communications channels exist on the Microsoft Office 365 project?

4.1 Project Performance Report: Microsoft Office 365

1035. To what degree does the teams purpose constitute a broader, deeper aspiration than just accomplishing short-term goals?

1036. To what degree can the team ensure that all members are individually and jointly accountable for the teams purpose, goals, approach, and work-products?

1037. How is the data used?

1038. To what degree will the team adopt a concrete, clearly understood, and agreed-upon approach that will result in achievement of the teams goals?

1039. What is the degree to which rules govern information exchange between groups?

1040. To what degree does the information network communicate information relevant to the task?

1041. To what degree do team members agree with the goals, relative importance, and the ways in which achievement will be measured?

1042. What degree are the relative importance and priority of the goals clear to all team members?

1043. To what degree do team members feel that the purpose of the team is important, if not exciting?

1044. To what degree are the skill areas critical to team performance present?

1045. To what degree are the structures of the formal organization consistent with the behaviors in the informal organization?

1046. To what degree does the formal organization make use of individual resources and meet individual needs?

1047. To what degree does the informal organization make use of individual resources and meet individual needs?

1048. To what degree are the tasks requirements reflected in the flow and storage of information?

1049. To what degree do members articulate the goals beyond the team membership?

1050. To what degree are the demands of the task compatible with and converge with the relationships of the informal organization?

1051. To what degree do the structures of the formal organization motivate taskrelevant behavior and facilitate task completion?

4.2 Variance Analysis: Microsoft Office 365

1052. How do you manage changes in the nature of the overhead requirements?

1053. What is the budgeted cost for work scheduled?

1054. Are all budgets assigned to control accounts?

1055. How does your organization measure performance?

1056. What are the direct labor dollars and/or hours?

1057. What is the performance to date and material commitment?

1058. Favorable or unfavorable variance?

1059. Wbs elements contractually specified for reporting of status to your organization (lowest level only)?

1060. Is the entire contract planned in time-phased control accounts to the extent practicable?

1061. The anticipated business volume?

1062. How does your organization allocate the cost of shared expenses and services?

1063. Does the accounting system provide a basis

for auditing records of direct costs chargeable to the contract?

1064. There are detailed schedules which support control account and work package start and completion dates/events?

1065. Can the relationship with problem customers be restructured so that there is a win-win situation?

1066. Are the requirements for all items of overhead established by rational, traceable processes?

1067. Are there quarterly budgets with quarterly performance comparisons?

1068. Are data elements reconcilable between internal summary reports and reports forwarded to the stakeholders?

1069. How does the use of a single conversion element (rather than the traditional labor and overhead elements) affect standard costing?

1070. What should management do?

4.3 Earned Value Status: Microsoft Office 365

1071. What is the unit of forecast value?

1072. How much is it going to cost by the finish?

1073. Verification is a process of ensuring that the developed system satisfies the stakeholders agreements and specifications; Are you building the product right? What do you haverify?

1074. Are you hitting your Microsoft Office 365 projects targets?

1075. If earned value management (EVM) is so good in determining the true status of a Microsoft Office 365 project and Microsoft Office 365 project its completion, why is it that hardly any one uses it in information systems related Microsoft Office 365 projects?

1076. Earned value can be used in almost any Microsoft Office 365 project situation and in almost any Microsoft Office 365 project environment. it may be used on large Microsoft Office 365 projects, medium sized Microsoft Office 365 projects, tiny Microsoft Office 365 projects (in cut-down form), complex and simple Microsoft Office 365 projects and in any market sector. some people, of course, know all about earned value, they have used it for years - but perhaps not as effectively as they could have?

1077. When is it going to finish?

1078. Validation is a process of ensuring that the developed system will actually achieve the stakeholders desired outcomes; Are you building the right product? What do you validate?

1079. Where is evidence-based earned value in your organization reported?

1080. Where are your problem areas?

1081. How does this compare with other Microsoft Office 365 projects?

4.4 Risk Audit: Microsoft Office 365

1082. Does your board meet regularly and document all decisions and actions?

1083. What events or circumstances could affect the achievement of your objectives?

1084. Do you record and file all audits?

1085. Does your organization have any policies or procedures to guide its decision-making (code of conduct for the board, conflict of interest policy, etc.)?

1086. Assessing risk with analytical procedures: do systemsthinking tools help auditors focus on diagnostic patterns?

1087. Are risk management strategies documented?

1088. Do requirements demand the use of new analysis, design, or testing methods?

1089. Do staff understand the extent of duty of care?

1090. How can the strategy fail/achieved?

1091. Do you have an emergency plan?

1092. Are all managers or operators of the facility or equipment competent or qualified?

1093. Have all involved been advised of any obligations they have to sponsors?

1094. Whence the business risk audit?

1095. For this risk .. what do you need to stop doing, start doing and keep doing?

1096. What are the costs associated with late delivery or a defective product?

1097. Are requirements fully understood by the team and customers?

1098. To what extent are auditors effective at linking business risks and management assertions?

1099. Does the implementation method matter?

4.5 Contractor Status Report: Microsoft Office 365

1100. What are the minimum and optimal bandwidth requirements for the proposed soluiton?

1101. If applicable; describe your standard schedule for new software version releases. Are new software version releases included in the standard maintenance plan?

1102. What process manages the contracts?

1103. Are there contractual transfer concerns?

1104. Who can list a Microsoft Office 365 project as organization experience, your organization or a previous employee of your organization?

1105. What is the average response time for answering a support call?

1106. What was the actual budget or estimated cost for your organizations services?

1107. Describe how often regular updates are made to the proposed solution. Are corresponding regular updates included in the standard maintenance plan?

1108. What was the budget or estimated cost for your organizations services?

1109. What was the final actual cost?

1110. What was the overall budget or estimated cost?

1111. How is risk transferred?

1112. How long have you been using the services?

1113. How does the proposed individual meet each requirement?

4.6 Formal Acceptance: Microsoft Office 365

1114. Was the Microsoft Office 365 project goal achieved?

1115. Was the sponsor/customer satisfied?

1116. Is formal acceptance of the Microsoft Office 365 project product documented and distributed?

1117. Do you buy-in installation services?

1118. How well did the team follow the methodology?

1119. Does it do what client said it would?

1120. General estimate of the costs and times to complete the Microsoft Office 365 project?

1121. What are the requirements against which to test, Who will execute?

1122. Was the Microsoft Office 365 project work done on time, within budget, and according to specification?

1123. How does your team plan to obtain formal acceptance on your Microsoft Office 365 project?

1124. What function(s) does it fill or meet?

1125. Do you perform formal acceptance or burn-in

tests?

1126. Do you buy pre-configured systems or build your own configuration?

1127. Was the Microsoft Office 365 project managed well?

1128. What can you do better next time?

1129. What lessons were learned about your Microsoft Office 365 project management methodology?

1130. What is the Acceptance Management Process?

1131. Have all comments been addressed?

1132. Was business value realized?

1133. Who supplies data?

5.0 Closing Process Group: Microsoft Office 365

1134. Is this a follow-on to a previous Microsoft Office 365 project?

1135. Measurable - are the targets measurable?

1136. What is the amount of funding and what Microsoft Office 365 project phases are funded?

1137. Were cost budgets met?

1138. What were things that you did very well and want to do the same again on the next Microsoft Office 365 project?

1139. What is the Microsoft Office 365 project name and date of completion?

1140. Did the Microsoft Office 365 project management methodology work?

1141. How well did the chosen processes fit the needs of the Microsoft Office 365 project?

1142. How well did the chosen processes produce the expected results?

1143. Who are the Microsoft Office 365 project stakeholders?

1144. How dependent is the Microsoft Office 365

project on other Microsoft Office 365 projects or work efforts?

1145. What can you do better next time, and what specific actions can you take to improve?

1146. Did the Microsoft Office 365 project team have enough people to execute the Microsoft Office 365 project plan?

1147. Does the close educate others to improve performance?

1148. What were the desired outcomes?

5.1 Procurement Audit: Microsoft Office 365

1149. Is the procurement function/unit organized the most appropriate way taking into consideration the actual tasks which the department has to carry out?

1150. Was the pre-qualification screening for issue of tender documents done properly and in a fair manner?

1151. Are all purchase orders signed by the purchasing agent?

1152. Are all checks pre-numbered?

1153. Does the procurement process compile basic procurement information such as how much is bought and spend with individual suppliers?

1154. How do you ensure whether the goods were supplied or works executed in time and properly recorded in measurement books and stock/works registers after inspection?

1155. Does the strategy ensure that the concepts of standardisation and coordination of procurement are used to take advantage of the departments collective buying power?

1156. Is it tested periodically, whether your organizations way of handling tasks is competitive in relation to price and quality?

1157. Is electronic procurement applied to reduce transaction costs?

1158. Does the individual approving disbursements sign or initial the document?

1159. Where required, were candidates registered as approved contractors, suppliers or service providers or certified by relevant bodies?

1160. Are there policies regarding special approval for capital expenditures?

1161. Are all complaints of late or incorrect payment sent to a person independent of the already stated having cash disbursement responsibilities?

1162. Are petty cash funds operated on an imprest basis?

1163. Does your organization maintain a current file of vendors and vendor catalogues?

1164. Is there no evidence that the expert has influenced the decisions taken by the public authority in his/her interest or in the interest of a specific contractor?

1165. Is the purchase order form clear and complete so that the vendor understands all terms and conditions?

1166. Are vendor price lists regularly updated?

1167. Has management taken the necessary steps to

ensure that relevant control systems are always up to date?

1168. Has it been determined which areas of procurement the audit should cover?

5.2 Contract Close-Out: Microsoft Office 365

1169. What happens to the recipient of services?

1170. Have all contract records been included in the Microsoft Office 365 project archives?

1171. Are the signers the authorized officials?

1172. What is capture management?

1173. Have all acceptance criteria been met prior to final payment to contractors?

1174. Change in knowledge?

1175. Was the contract complete without requiring numerous changes and revisions?

1176. Was the contract type appropriate?

1177. Change in attitude or behavior?

1178. Have all contracts been completed?

1179. How is the contracting office notified of the automatic contract close-out?

1180. Parties: who is involved?

1181. Was the contract sufficiently clear so as not to result in numerous disputes and misunderstandings?

1182. Parties: Authorized?

1183. How does it work?

1184. Change in circumstances?

1185. How/when used ?

1186. Have all contracts been closed?

1187. Has each contract been audited to verify acceptance and delivery?

5.3 Project or Phase Close-Out: Microsoft Office 365

1188. Who exerted influence that has positively affected or negatively impacted the Microsoft Office 365 project?

1189. What were the goals and objectives of the communications strategy for the Microsoft Office 365 project?

1190. Have business partners been involved extensively, and what data was required for them?

1191. Is the lesson based on actual Microsoft Office 365 project experience rather than on independent research?

1192. Does the lesson educate others to improve performance?

1193. How much influence did the stakeholder have over others?

1194. Was the schedule met?

1195. Were messages directly related to the release strategy or phases of the Microsoft Office 365 project?

1196. What is a Risk Management Process?

1197. What security considerations needed to be addressed during the procurement life cycle?

1198. Were the outcomes different from the already stated planned?

1199. What information did each stakeholder need to contribute to the Microsoft Office 365 projects success?

1200. Who is responsible for award close-out?

1201. What could have been improved?

1202. What was expected from each stakeholder?

1203. Is there a clear cause and effect between the activity and the lesson learned?

1204. What advantages do the an individual interview have over a group meeting, and vice-versa?

5.4 Lessons Learned: Microsoft Office 365

1205. Was the Microsoft Office 365 project manager sufficiently experienced, skilled, trained, supported?

1206. How useful was the content of the training you received in preparation for the use of the product/service?

1207. How effective was Microsoft Office 365 project Team member training?

1208. Was there enough support – guidance, clerical support, training?

1209. How objective was the collection of data?

1210. Was the Microsoft Office 365 project significantly delayed/hampered by outside dependencies (outside to the Microsoft Office 365 project, that is)?

1211. Is there any way in which you think your development process hampered this Microsoft Office 365 project?

1212. How effectively were issues resolved before escalation was necessary?

1213. If you had to do this Microsoft Office 365 project again, what is the one thing that you would change (related to process, not to technical solutions)?

1214. How timely were Progress Reports provided to the Microsoft Office 365 project Manager by Team Members?

1215. How useful was the format and content of the Microsoft Office 365 project Status Report to you?

1216. How was the Microsoft Office 365 project controlled?

1217. How adequately involved did you feel in Microsoft Office 365 project decisions?

1218. Was the change control process properly implemented to manage changes to cost, scope, schedule, or quality?

1219. How actively and meaningfully were stakeholders involved in the Microsoft Office 365 project?

1220. How clear were you on your role in the Microsoft Office 365 project?

1221. Is the lesson significant, valid, and applicable?

1222. What regulatory regime controlled how your organization head and program manager directed your organization and Microsoft Office 365 project?

1223. How effective were the communications materials in providing and orienting team members about the details of the Microsoft Office 365 project?

1224. If issue escalation was required, how effectively

were issues resolved?

Index

289

nervous   143
network   3, 48, 110, 164-165, 240
Neutral 12, 17, 27, 41, 55, 67, 80, 91
normal 87, 155, 206
Notice 1
noticing   224
notified   257
notify   231
number   26, 40, 48, 54, 66, 79, 90, 126, 160, 170, 190, 264
numbers   104
numerous   257
objective   7, 45, 131, 133, 136, 197, 238, 261
objectives   22, 24, 27, 31, 37, 59-60, 84, 88, 93, 111, 114, 116,
138, 157, 169, 181, 183-184, 199, 206-207, 217, 228, 233, 246, 259
observe   191
observed   75
observing   150
obsolete   125
obstacles   18, 172, 179
obtain 110, 250
obtained   40-41, 142
obvious   110
obviously   13
occurrence   220
occurring   70
occurs 21, 89, 128-129, 136, 185, 226
offerings   63, 71
Office 1-6, 9-15, 17-20, 22-40, 42-43, 45-49, 51-54, 56-66, 68-69,
71-80, 82-114, 116-123, 125-128, 130-136, 138-144, 146, 148-154,
156-160, 162, 164, 166-183, 185, 187, 189, 191-195, 197-199, 201-
205, 207-209, 211-213, 215-221, 223, 225, 228, 230, 232, 234, 236,
238-240, 242, 244-246, 248, 250-254, 257, 259-262
officials 257
offline 59
offset   51
OneDrive   59, 65
one-time   7
ongoing   44, 88, 158, 171
online 11, 123
on-site 228
operate   181, 205, 220
operated   255
operates   115

291

Lightning Source UK Ltd.
Milton Keynes UK
UKHW040157060119
334993UK00018B/567/P